# BaCK to BaSiCS

# Back to Basics

## THE EDUCATION YOU WISH YOU'D HAD

## CAROLINE TAGGART

MICHAEL O'MARA BOOKS LIMITED

This paperback edition first published in 2017

First published in Great Britain in 2012 by
Michael O'Mara Books Limited
9 Lion Yard
Tremadoc Road
London SW4 7NQ

A CIP catalogue record for this book is available from the British
Library.

Papers used by Michael O'Mara Books Limited are natural, recyclable
products made from wood grown in sustainable forests. The
manufacturing processes conform to the environmental regulations of the
country of origin.

ISBN: 978-1-78243-781-9 in paperback print format
ISBN: 978-1-84317-900-9 in ePub format
ISBN: 978-1-84317-899-6 in Mobipocket format

1 2 3 4 5 6 7 8 9 10

Designed and typeset by K.DESIGN, Winscombe, Somerset
Illustrations by Greg Stevenson

Printed and bound by CPI Group (UK) Ltd, Croydon, CR0 4YY

www.mombooks.com

# Contents

# Introduction

Have you ever been embarrassed – in a discussion with friends, in front of the children, watching a quiz programme on television – by not knowing the answer to something that seems absolutely basic? By not being sure what a prime number is or the difference between climate and weather or conduction and convection?

No? Well, put this book straight back on the shelf. You already know everything it could possibly tell you.

Changed your mind? How nice! It's good to have you on board.

The truth is, we've all been there. We were taught all sorts of stuff at school but have forgotten it; or – increasingly likely in my case, and particularly where Science and Geography are concerned – it's been invented, discovered or changed since we left school and we've never quite got to grips with it. This book aims to fill in some of the gaps in knowledge we really feel we ought to have.

It's divided into chapters along the lines of subjects you may have studied for GCSE or O Level – English Language, Maths, Science, History, French, Geography and General Studies – but that is as close as it comes to following a syllabus. Science covers seemingly random concepts such as why yeast makes dough rise and why helium is good in balloons, because that's the sort of thing that will make you feel silly if you can't explain it to a five-year-old. Maths helps you to divide the bill in a restaurant and has a go at working out how the bank calculates the interest on your mortgage. Geography explains the difference between latitude and longitude and why it matters, because if you are a high-flying executive permanently battling jet-lag, it might just be a comfort to know what is happening to you. History is a run-down of a lot of things that have happened in the world since 1453 – no mean feat in thirty pages, but it also gives you a chance to remind yourself (or look up and find out) why indeed you should care about what happened in 1453.

French sheds light on the mysteries of irregular verbs and why the words for inanimate objects have a gender. The General Studies chapter allows you to take on board the difference between a sonata and a symphony, not to mention a Doric column and a Gothic arch. And English – well, English goes back to that perennial question of why we speak, write, spell and put in apostrophes the way we do.

In other words, as the subtitle boasts, it is the education you wish you'd had. It isn't what they didn't teach you at Harvard Business School; it probably won't enable you to win friends or influence people; but it will make you more confident in expressing an opinion on subjects from oxbow lakes to oxymorons, from hyperbole to Helen of Troy. Which, for many of us, is all that matters.

Caroline Taggart

# Acknowledgements

Writing a book like this makes you only too aware of the gaps in your own education. So I am particularly grateful to Heather, Hilary and Marianne, respectively geographer, historian and scientist *extraordinaires*, who filled in the calderas and black holes in my knowledge. Thanks also to Katie, Toby, Ana, Jess and the rest of the MOM team, without whom ...

# ENGLISH LANGUAGE

It's beautiful, rich and diverse, but there is no denying that it is full of strange rules and even stranger exceptions. It pronounces *bough*, *rough*, *cough* and *through* so that they don't rhyme and *jerk*, *dirk*, *work* and *murk* so that they do. In other words, it's a minefield. This chapter tries to throw light on some of the most frequent areas of confusion.

## MY HUSBAND AND ... WHO?

One of the things that people find hardest about English is the correct use of pronouns. After all, if the Queen says, 'My husband and I ...', it must be right, mustn't it?

But no, not necessarily. It all depends on where in the sentence it comes. Let's look at the rules.

### Sentence structure: subject, verb and object

A basic English sentence consists of a subject, a verb and an object:

- The subject **performs the action** of the sentence.

- The verb tell us **what the action is**.

- The object is **the recipient of the action**.

Easier with a few examples, perhaps:

*The dog chased the ball.*
*I am reading a book.*
*Old Macdonald had a farm.*

The subjects of these sentences are *the dog*, *I* and *Old Macdonald*. They are the ones that are doing something. You'll remember, I'm sure, that a verb is a 'doing word', so the verbs in these sentences are *chased*, *am reading* and *had*: they describe the action that is taking place. The objects are *the ball*, *a book* and *a farm*. Ask yourself 'The dog chased what?' and the answer will be the object of the verb.

OK? With me so far? Good.

## Pronouns

Pronouns are the little words that stand in place of nouns, to save us having to repeat the nouns over and over again. It would be tedious, for example, to say:

> *Caroline is writing Caroline's book because Caroline has agreed to write the book.*

Instead, we substitute pronouns:

> *Caroline is writing* her *book because* she *has agreed to write* it.

English does not alter the form of nouns to show what role they play in a sentence (as Latin and German, for instance, do), but it does alter the form of pronouns:

> *I* as the subject of a sentence becomes *me* as the object.

*He* becomes *him.*
*She* becomes *her.*
*We* becomes *us.*
*They* becomes *them.*

Thus:

I *hit the ball; the ball hit* me.
He *doesn't wear green; green doesn't suit* him.
She *isn't going to the party; nobody invited* her.
We *don't own a dog; dogs frighten* us.
They *go on holiday at Christmas; it relaxes* them.

Note that *you* and *it* remain the same whether they are subject or object:

You *like dancing; dancing pleases* you.
It *was lying on the table; John saw* it.

## Compounds

The complication arises when you have what is called a *compound subject* or *compound object*: that is, one that includes more than one element. Think back to 'my husband and I' and remember the difference between a subject and an object:

*My husband and I* are very grateful for the invitation.
Thank you for inviting *my husband and me.*

### If in doubt ...

If you are ever in doubt about which version is correct, put a mental bracket around 'my husband and'. You wouldn't dream of saying, 'Thank you for inviting I', would you? So you shouldn't say, 'Thank you for inviting my husband and I' either.

Here are a few more examples. I've put in those imaginary brackets, in the hope of being helpful.

> They [and their father] *were at loggerheads.*
> *There was disagreement between* [their father and] them.

> We [and the Germans] *fought in the Second World War.*
> *The Second World War was a conflict involving* [the Germans and] us.

> They [and their children] *are coming for the weekend.*
> *I have to go to the station to meet* them [and their children].

It works when there are two pronouns too.

> She and I *would love to come.*
> *Please buy tickets for* her and me.

In the first sentence, you can put your brackets round either 'she and' or 'and I' and the rule applies. Similarly in the second sentence with 'her and' or 'and me'.

## Overemphasis

Still on the subject of pronouns, another common error is the misuse of emphatic ones. Words ending in *–self* or *–selves –*

*myself*, *yourself*, *themselves*, etc. – are used reflexively, when *you* did something to *yourself*, i.e. when the subject is the same as the object:

> *I dressed* myself *in a hurry because I was running late.*
> *He took* himself *severely to task after he had lost his temper.*

There isn't generally any problem in this context. But difficulties can arise in relation to the other role of these pronouns – emphasis.

The following examples show emphatic pronouns being used correctly:

> Myself, *I love living in the country*
> (although I know that you find it dull).

> *We can find the way* ourselves
> (so we don't need directions).

> *I want you all to do this homework* yourselves
> (rather than getting your parents to help you or copying it from Wikipedia).

What is wrong, or at best unnecessary, is to use this form when there is no need for emphasis. It's a trick much loved by people at call centres. 'The documents will be sent to yourself today,' they say, meaning nothing more than 'The documents will be sent to you.' There's no question (we hope) of their sending the documents to anyone else, so there's no need to labour the fact.

The point here is that using an emphatic word when no

emphasis is intended weakens it. In the example above, if enough people use 'yourself' when they mean 'you', it will become the norm – and then what will yourselves do when you want to be emphatic?

## TO APOSTROPHIZE OR NOT TO APOSTROPHIZE

Many people get into a panic about apostrophes but there is really no need. Honestly.

By and large, apostrophes are used for two reasons:

- To show that something is missing.

- To indicate possession.

### Something missing

When something is missing, it is most commonly the *o* in *not*, which produces words such as *don't*, *won't* and *shan't*. *Won't* and *shan't*, of course, are short for *will not* and *shall not*, but don't be lured into thinking that you need more than one apostrophe: the convention is that the apostrophe replaces the missing *o* and nothing else.

An apostrophe also often replaces the *i* of *is* or the *a* of *are*:

He's (= he is) *a charming man.*
They're (= they are) *a peculiar couple.*

### Possession

As for possession, if you want to show that something belongs to someone or something, add an apostrophe and an *s*:

> *Tom's first birthday*
> *The doctor's bag*
> *The mirror's gilt frame*

## Possessive plurals

If it belongs to persons or things whose plural form ends in *s,* just add an apostrophe:

> *The sisters' rivalry* (when there is more than one sister)
> *The teachers' day off* (more than one teacher)

If it is a plural but doesn't end in *s,* add an apostrophe and an *s*:

> *The children's shoes*
> *The blind mice's tails*

And if it is becoming a bit of a mouthful or just doesn't sound right, rephrase it:

> *The rivalry between the sisters*
> *The tails of the blind mice*

## Abbreviations

There is no need to put an apostrophe in the plural of an abbreviation, unless it is to show possession:

> *I am buying everyone DVDs for Christmas.*
> *That DVD's sound quality is dreadful.*
> *Those DVDs' covers are very striking.*

There are other refinements, but you won't go too far wrong if you stick to these rules.

## An exception to the rule ...

But just when you thought we had finished with pronouns, there is another important rule: **possessive pronouns do not have an apostrophe**:

> *The dog gnawed at* its *bone.*
> Hers *is the most glamorous dress in the room.*
> *I didn't know you were a friend of* theirs.

*Her's*, *your's*, *our's*, *their's* simply do not exist. The one to be careful about is *its*, because *it's* does exist: but is short for *it is*:

> *The cat is waving* its *tail, so you can tell that* it's *cross*.

**Who's there?**

Following on from *its* and *it's*, here are two other groups of words that look or sound similar but are used in different ways:

> Who's *there?* (short for 'who is' – note the apostrophe indicating the missing *i*)

> Whose *gloves are these?*
> (meaning 'to whom do they belong?')

> There *are very few presents under the tree over* there (indicating place or position).

> There's *no cause for alarm*
> (short for 'there is').

Their *presents will arrive at the last minute*
('belonging to them').

Theirs *are worth waiting for*
(a possessive pronoun, so no apostrophe).

They're *always late doing their shopping*
(short for 'they are').

## THAT SUPERMARKET BUSINESS –
## 'FEWER' OR 'LESS'?

The fuss about 'five items or less' is a bit of a chestnut, but it still confuses people, so how does it work?

In English we have things called countable and non-countable nouns. Not rocket science: if it is something you can count – *one penny*, *two sheep*, *three buckets* – it's a *countable* noun. You can also count these things in a vague way: *a few pence*, *many sheep*. If you are making a comparison, you say *fewer pence*, *more sheep*.

But you can't count snow, say, or beauty or baking powder: you have to say 'a little', 'a lot of' rather than one, two or three. These are *non-countable* nouns. With a comparison, you don't say 'fewer snow', 'fewer beauty' – you use the word *less*.

So the rule is simple:

- With countable nouns, use *fewer*.

- With non-countable nouns, use *less*.

In both instances, you say *more* when you mean – well, more, but that shouldn't cause you a problem in the average supermarket.

## COMPARATIVES AND SUPERLATIVES

When you are making a comparison, as in the *less/fewer* example above, you are comparing two things (or two sets of things) and *no more than two*. Once you have three things or more, you need to use a superlative.

Comparatives often end in –*er*: *bigger, prettier, happier.*

The equivalent superlatives end in –*est*: *biggest, prettiest, happiest.* So:

> *Our new house is* bigger *than the old one.*
> *It is the* biggest *house we have ever lived in.*
>
> *She is* prettier *than her sister.*
> *She is the* prettiest *of the three sisters.*
>
> *I am* happier *in my new job.*
> *This is the* happiest *I have been in years.*

With longer words use *more* to form a comparative, *most* to form a superlative. To indicate a reduction or a negative comparison, use *less* or *least*, even with a short adjective:

> *The Natural History Museum seems* more interesting *every time I visit it.*
> *That is the* most interesting *exhibit in the museum.*
>
> *She is* less timid *than she was six months ago.*
> *That is the* least helpful *helpline I have ever spoken to.*

## An exception to the rule

The comparatives and superlatives of *good* are formed in an irregular way: the comparatives are *better* and *worse* and their equivalent superlatives *best* and *worst*:

> *She is a* good *tennis player.*
> *She is* better *at tennis than her brother.*
> *She is the* best *tennis player in the club.*

> *He has* bad *manners.*
> *His manners are* worse *than mine.*
> *He has the* worst *manners of anyone I know.*

# TO SPLIT OR NOT TO SPLIT

Over the years there has been a very great deal of debate over whether or not an infinitive may be split. And I think you'll agree that it's easier to have an opinion if you know (and care) what an infinitive is.

It's the form of a verb that you can put *to* in front of: *to compare*, *to dance*, *to appreciate*. It's *infinite* because it doesn't indicate singular or plural or past or future or anything of that sort. It just expresses the *idea* of the verb. Purists maintain that you should never put a word between the *to* and the rest of the verb: *Star Trek*'s 'to boldly go' is the clichéd example. Modern fashion asserts that this is a nonsensical piece of pedantry and that avoiding splitting an infinitive often sounds awkward and contrived.

## What to do?

So is it better meticulously to avoid splitting an infinitive, to meticulously avoid splitting an infinitive or to avoid splitting an infinitive meticulously? Our purists would undoubtedly opt for the first; modern fashion would shrug its shoulders and say that the second was fine. Both, I should hope, would purse their lips at the third, but for a different reason. A good rule of thumb with adverbs is to put them as close as possible to the word that they qualify. This helps to avoid ambiguity and unintentional humour. In the last example, the position of 'meticulously' makes it sound as if you are being meticulous about the splitting rather than the avoiding, which is just silly.

Want me to be dogmatic? OK, I tend more and more towards the modern, shoulder-shrugging view. Does it sound right with the infinitive split? Would the alternative be clumsy? That, to me, is more important than clinging limpet-like to an eighteenth-century rule.

## A SPELLING BEE

At primary school we were given lists of words to learn and then tested on their spelling the next day. But we were young then – we had memories. In theory, if I set myself to learn twenty words a day, it would take me about eighteen months to master the average person's working vocabulary of 10,000 words. In practice it would take something nearer fourteen years, because I would routinely forget eighteen out of the twenty and have to do them again. So let's try to make it easier by imposing a few rules and aide-memoires (and if you don't know what an aide-memoire is, skip ahead to page 29).

## Practice/practise, licence/license?

In British English (though not in American), where confusion in spelling involves the question '*c* or *s*'?, the answer is '*c* for a noun, *s* for a verb'. The easiest way to remember this is to remember a common pairing where the words are pronounced differently:

> *If you take my* advice, *you'll go to bed early.*
> *I* advise *you to listen to him.*

That should enable you to extrapolate and apply the same rule to other pairs that are pronounced differently, such as *device/ devise* or *prophecy/prophesy*, and to those that are pronounced the same, such as *practice/practise* and *licence/ license.*

> *How did you* devise *such a cunning* device?
> *I* prophesy *that this will end in disaster, and my* prophecies *always come true.*
> *A lawyer's* practice *enables him to* practise *law.*
> *A driving* licence licenses *you to drive a car.*

## I before e ...

The most common spelling memory aid is, of course, 'i before e except after c'. I always feel it is of limited use, because you have to remember that it works only when the *ie* or *ei* is pronounced 'ee'. So it helps with:

*achieve*

*aggrieve*

*believe*    (and *belief,* even though the pronunciation differs)

*deceive*

*grieve*

*niece*

*receipt*

*receive*

*reprieve*

*retrieve*

*shriek*

*siege*

*wield*

*yield*

and doubtless many others. But even when you apply the pronunciation restriction, *caffeine*, *codeine*, *protein* and *seize* are exceptions. The rule doesn't help at all with words where the *ei* is pronounced in some other way, such as *Fräulein*, *skein* or *villein* or where the *e* and *i* are part of separate syllables, as in *fancier* or *wherein*.

## Some more spelling aids

There are lots of other 'tricks' for remembering difficult spellings:

**desert/dessert:** remember that the sweet one has two sugars (two esses).

24

**embarrass** (double r and double s):  do you go *Really Red And Smile Shyly* when embarrassed?

**fulfil:** 'full' and 'fill', but with only one l in each.

**jewellery** is made by a jeweller.

**stationery** is sold by a stationer.

**weather/whether:** *we* look *at her* (the weather girl) to find out *whether* or not it is going to rain.

But frankly a lot of these supposed aids are so convoluted that you are better off looking the words up in a dictionary if you need to know how to spell them – and reading as widely as you can so that you become familiar with them.

## Some spelling pitfalls

To get you started, here is a list of some commonly misspelt words. Note that, as with the examples above, a lot of the problems concern whether or not to duplicate a letter, and most of the rest are about which vowel to use when it's in a syllable that tends to be mumbled:

> *a**cco**mm**o**dation*
> *bro**cco**li*
> *cem**eter**y*
> *commi**tt**ee*
> *defi**n**ite*
> *delicat**essen***
> *d**i**lapidated*
> *gu**ara**ntee*

*idiosyncrasy* (but *aristocracy*, *bureaucracy*,
*democracy*)

*liaison*

*maintenance*

*manoeuvre*

*mantelpiece*

*necessary*

*parallel*

*soliloquy*

*supersede*

*threshold*

*vacuum*

*withhold*

If you knew how to spell all of those, good for you. Try these:

*avocado*

*beleaguered*

*calendar*

*caster sugar*

*colander*

*connoisseur*

*dysfunctional*

*ecstasy*

*extrovert*

*facetious*

*guerrilla*

*linchpin*

*margarine*

*memento*

*phosphorus*

*putr**e**fy*
*questio**nn**aire*
*sku**ld**u**gg**ery*
*t**ee**tota**ll**er*
*va**cc**inate*

Spellchecks help a lot, but they can't necessarily tell you that you have made the right choice between *calendar* and *colander*, *gorilla* and *guerrilla* or *linchpin* and *lynch mob*. If you are checking something you have written, read it through yourself and make sure you have used the right word, not the wrong one spelt correctly. And note the use of *yourself*, the emphatic pronoun, in that last sentence (see page 14).

## –able/–ible/–ance/–ence?

The sad truth is that there is no reliable rule to tell you which spelling to use. To be confident, you have not only to know Latin and Greek but also have an idea of how the Latin or Greek root evolved into English. Also there are sometimes nuances in meaning between spellings: a woman with small children, for example, may be said to have *dependants*, but these *dependants* are *dependent* on her. Did I mention that English was a minefield? Here's a list of some words with these endings, but really, again, a good dictionary is the only reliable solution.

### –able

*adaptable*
*admirable*
*available*

### –ible

*admissible*
*audible*
*contemptible*

believable

debatable

fashionable

favourable

indispensable

negotiable

obtainable

readable

remarkable

valuable

variable

venerable

convertible

digestible

edible

fallible

flexible

horrible

incredible

irresistible

legible

negligible

terrible

visible

## –ant

applicant

assistant

consultant

defendant

expectant

extravagant

exuberant

itinerant

observant

reluctant

significant

vigilant

## –ent

belligerent

coherent

competent

consistent

deficient

different

excellent

independent

non-existent

resident

sufficient

urgent

Nouns derived from these adjectives follow the same pattern:
*expectancy, extravagance, coherence, deficiency*, etc.

# WHY DO WE SAY ...?

English is always described as the richest language in the world, and one of the reasons for this is that we have 'borrowed' so enthusiastically from other languages. I put 'borrowed' in inverted commas because I haven't heard any suggestion that we are going to give these words back.

Anyway, foreign terms that we use almost without thinking about where they come from include:

**Aide-memoire:** French, 'help for the memory'. Something to remind you of what you have to do, such as notes for a speech or leaving the rubbish by the back door so that you don't forget to take it out.

**Carte blanche:** French, 'white or blank card'. If you have a blank card you can write what you like on it, so you have complete power to do – well, anything, really. If you were to give a caterer *carte blanche* over your party, for example, you would leave them to choose the menu and let the budget take care of itself. Quite a risky thing to do.

**Et cetera:** Latin, 'and other things'. We use this to mean 'and so on and so on', often *ad nauseam* (to the point of being sick of it) or even *ad infinitum* (for ever and ever, until infinity).

**Fait accompli:** French, 'accomplished fact'. To present someone with a *fait accompli* is to do something without asking their permission, so as to give them no chance to object.

**Faux pas:** French, 'false step'. We use it more in a social, conversational sense – you might make a *faux pas* by mentioning someone's ex in front of their new partner.

**Gravitas:** Latin, 'heaviness'. Again, we use this metaphorically, to mean seriousness of character and behaviour, particularly the sort of seriousness that is appropriate to a job or position. You need a certain *gravitas* to be a judge, for example, or to play Othello.

**Idée fixe:** French, 'fixed idea'. Something that you can't get out of your head, an obsession.

**Incommunicado:** Spanish, 'cut off, isolated'. Once upon a time this was likely to mean 'in solitary confinement'; now it could describe someone you texted half an hour ago who hasn't answered.

**Je ne sais quoi:** French, 'I don't know what'. In English usage almost always preceded by the words 'a certain', meaning 'a certain something, a certain stylishness'.

**Non sequitur:** Latin, 'it doesn't follow'. We use this as a noun to describe *something* that doesn't follow, in a logical sense: it is a non sequitur to claim that because you studied Physics at school you are capable of designing a space rocket.

**Pied-à-terre:** French, 'foot on the ground'; idiomatically a flat, usually in London, where you can stay when your work or your need for a therapeutic visit to Harvey Nichols makes it inconvenient for you to go back to the country mansion to sleep.

**Status quo:** Latin, 'the condition in which'. In English this applies to 'the current state of affairs', often one that is less than ideal but has to be endured.

# A GLOSSARY OF LITERARY TERMS

Writers use various devices to make their words sound more effective; poets write in different forms and formats, which have technical names. Here's an explanation of some of the most frequently used terms.

**Alliteration:** using a number of words that begin with the same sound.

**Blank verse:** a term that can be applied to any verse that doesn't rhyme, but is used specifically to describe the iambic pentameters in the plays of Shakespeare and in Milton's *Paradise Lost*. In this context, a scene or a stanza may end with a rhyming couplet.

**Epic poetry:** is by definition long and concerns the exploits of a legendary hero, such as Odysseus in Homer's *Odyssey* or Beowulf in the anonymous Anglo-Saxon poem of the same name.

**Epigram:** a short and witty saying, of the kind perfected by Oscar Wilde ('I can resist everything except temptation.'). Not to be confused with an **epitaph**, the words written on a gravestone, or an **epigraph**, a quotation at the beginning of a book or chapter, suggesting its theme.

**Euphemism:** a turn of phrase that avoids saying something unpleasant. 'Passed away' is a euphemism for 'died'.

**Foot:** in poetic terms, this is a unit of two or three syllables repeated over and over again with the same stress pattern. Different stress patterns have different names: a long or stressed syllable followed by a short one is a *trochee*; the reverse, a short syllable followed by a long one, is *iambic*; and a pattern of long followed by two shorts is a *dactyl*. Much of Shakespeare's verse is written in *iambic pentameters*: that is, each line consists of five iambic feet (ten syllables in all). Count them:

> *Once more unto the breach, dear friends, once more*
> *To sleep: perchance to dream: ay, there's the rub*
> *The quality of mercy is not strained*

It happens a lot.

**Hyperbole:** exaggeration for effect, as in 'I must have told you a thousand times'.

**Metaphor:** a figure of speech which says that something *is* something else when, in the literal sense, it isn't. If you say to someone, 'Aren't you a busy bee?', you are using the expression metaphorically – you are not suggesting that they have sprouted yellow and black stripes and learnt to fly.

**Metre:** the specific form of rhythm that makes up a line of verse, usually composed of a number of *feet* (see above). Confusingly, when you talk about a *pentameter* (having five feet), a *hexameter* (having six), etc., it is spelt *–meter*.

**Onomatopoeia:** a word, phrase or line of verse that reproduces the sound it is trying to convey: words such as *woof*, *meow* and *neigh* are all onomatopoeic.

**Oxymoron:** *tragicomedy*, *bitter sweet* – the juxtaposition for effect of two apparently contradictory words. *Virtual reality* is a more modern example.

**Quatrain:** a stanza or poem of four lines.

**Simile:** a comparison that, unlike a metaphor, acknowledges that it is a comparison, usually with the words *like* or *as*: *as busy as a bee*, *as cunning as a fox*, *like a dog with two tails*.

**Sonnet:** a poem of fourteen lines, written in iambic pentameters and with a specific rhyming scheme. The Shakespearean sonnet (and he wrote over 150 of them) always ends with two lines that rhyme, known as a *rhyming couplet*.

**Stanza:** a group of lines of verse following a set metrical pattern; the unit into which a poem is subdivided.

# MATHS

The problem with maths, as I recall it from school, was that you spent a lot of time proving that there were 180° in a triangle and making sense of equations such as $a^2 + b^2 = c^2$, but that no one bothered to explain why you needed to know these things. With that in mind, this chapter is going to concentrate largely on the elements of maths that are of use to most of us in everyday life. I'm going to assume that you know your times tables and can do simple sums: if not (and I'm sorry, purists, I hear your pain), feel free to dig out a calculator at any stage.

## (JUST A FEW) ARITHMETICAL BASICS ...

Even simple sums require a bit of specialist vocabulary, so let's start there.

The four basic functions in arithmetic are **addition**, **subtraction**, **multiplication** and **division**:

**Addition:** when you add two or more numbers together, you get the **sum** of those numbers.

**Subtraction:** subtract one number from another and the answer is the **difference** between them.

**Multiplication:** multiply two or more numbers together and the answer is the **product**.

**Division:** divide one number (the **divisor**) into another (the **dividend**) and the answer is a **quotient**. If the divisor does not go into the dividend an exact number of times, what is left over is the **remainder**.

Subtraction is addition in reverse and division is multiplication in reverse. For example, $4 + 8 = 12$. Reverse the process, by subtracting the 8 from 12 and you are back with 4.

Similarly,                    $4 \times 8 = 32$
Reverse the process:      $32 \div 8 = 4$

It works with larger numbers too. That's one of the beauties of maths: once you have established a principle, it holds true with any numbers you care to think of.

With addition and multiplication, the order you put the numbers in doesn't matter ($3 + 4$ is the same as $4 + 3$; $2 \times 7$ is the same as $7 \times 2$). With subtraction and division it does matter ($7 - 2$ is not the same as $2 - 7$, nor is $10 \div 2$ the same as $2 \div 10$).

Most numbers that we deal with in real life are **positive**, that is, they are larger than zero. If you subtract a larger number from a smaller one (as in $2 - 7$), you end up with a **negative** number ($-5$). When you did 'problems' at school and deducted 7 apples from 2 apples, the resulting $-5$ apples were of academic interest only. However, try putting £200 into the bank and then withdrawing £700 – you'll soon see that this has a real-life implication.

## ... AND A MEMORY AID

Not all calculations are as simple as the examples above. When they become complicated, it is often tempting to scream, 'Where do I start?' The thing to have at your fingertips at this point is BIDMAS, which stands for:

Brackets
Indices
Division
Multiplication
Addition
Subtraction

This is the order in which functions are performed. Imagine you are faced with:

$$6 \times (20 - 14)^3 + 72$$

It may seem unlikely, but never mind that. BIDMAS tells you that you do the brackets first $(20 - 14 = 6)$ and then the indices (in this case, the little raised 3 after the bracket). As we will see on page 49, that 3 means multiplying the bracket by itself three times: $(20 - 14)^3$ becomes $6 \times 6 \times 6 = 216$.

The sum is suddenly much simpler:

$$6 \times 216 + 72$$

Multiplication first:

$$6 \times 216 = 1296$$

Then finally addition:

$$1296 + 72 = 1368$$

Notice the importance of this: if, having reached $6 \times 216 + 72$, you then did the addition first, your answer would be $6 \times 288 = 1728$. Not the same thing at all.

## FRACTIONS, DECIMALS AND PERCENTAGES

These are all ways of expressing much the same thing: a quantity that is not a whole number.

### Fractions

Fractions (which should strictly be called vulgar fractions) are things like ½, ⅓, ⅖, ¾, in which one number (the **numerator**) is written above a line and the other (the **denominator**) is written below it. The denominator tells us what portion of the whole we are dealing with (a half, a third, a fifth, a quarter), while the numerator tells us how many of them there are (one, two, three). A whole number expressed as a fraction has a denominator of 1; thus ³⁄₁ is the same as 3.

### Doing sums with fractions

If you want to add or subtract fractions, they need to have a **common denominator** – the same number below the line in each case. To achieve this, you need to know that when you multiply or divide a numerator and a denominator by the same number, the value of the fraction remains the same: ½ is the same as ²⁄₄ or ³⁄₆ or ⁴⁄₈ and so on. A common denominator of two fractions can be found by multiplying the two denominators together. Thus to add ½ to ⅓, convert both fractions to sixths, 6 being the result of multiplying 2 by 3. (And remember to multiply the numerator by the same number too.) This gives:

$$\tfrac{3}{6} + \tfrac{2}{6} = \tfrac{5}{6}$$

If the numerator is larger than the denominator, the number is larger than 1. This is known as an **improper fraction**, and you obviously don't want that. Divide the denominator into the numerator to get a more decorous result:

$$\tfrac{3}{6} + \tfrac{4}{6} = \tfrac{7}{6} = 1\tfrac{1}{6}$$

Exactly the same thing happens with subtraction:

$$\tfrac{1}{2} - \tfrac{1}{3} \text{ becomes } \tfrac{3}{6} - \tfrac{2}{6} = \tfrac{1}{6}$$

Multiplication is easier: multiply the numerators, then multiply the denominators:

$$\tfrac{1}{2} \times \tfrac{1}{3} = \tfrac{1}{6}$$

For division, remember that this is the reverse of multiplication, so that to divide by $\tfrac{1}{3}$ is the same as to multiply by 3 (or $\tfrac{3}{1}$). Thus:

$$\tfrac{1}{2} \div \tfrac{1}{3} = \tfrac{1}{2} \times \tfrac{3}{1} = \tfrac{3}{2} = 1\tfrac{1}{2}$$

## Simplifying fractions

It's normal when dealing with fractions to express them in the simplest possible form, which means having the smallest possible numerator. So a fraction such as $\tfrac{4}{8}$ is **cancelled down**: you divide the numerator and denominator by 4 (because you can see at a glance that 4 divides evenly into both 4 and 8) to leave $\frac{1}{2}$. Similarly, with $\frac{5}{20}$, divide both elements by 5 to leave $\frac{1}{4}$. A fraction with a numerator of 1 is always in its simplest form, though $\frac{2}{5}$, $\frac{3}{4}$ and $\frac{17}{21}$ are also as neat and tidy as you can get.

## Decimals

Decimals or **decimal fractions** are fractions expressed with a **decimal point** rather than a numerator and a denominator: 0.5, 2.25, 3.142, etc.

With a whole number – 1782, for example – the right-hand digit represents the units, the one to the left of it the tens, then the hundreds and so on, so that 1782 is made up of 2 units + 8 tens + 7 hundreds + 1 thousand. With numbers after the decimal point this works in reverse: so 1.5 is $1 + \frac{5}{10}$, or $1\frac{1}{2}$; 2.25 is $2 + \frac{2}{10} + \frac{5}{100}$, or $2 + \frac{25}{100}$, or $2\frac{1}{4}$; 3.142 (pi, which we will hear more about later) is $3 + \frac{142}{1000}$ or approximately $3\frac{1}{7}$.

### Adding and subtracting decimals

Adding and subtracting decimals is exactly the same as adding and subtracting whole numbers: all you have to remember to do is align the decimal points. Thus:

$$
\begin{array}{r}
1.45 \\
+ \ \underline{2.34} \\
\underline{3.79}
\end{array}
$$

### Multiplying decimals

With multiplication, do the sum in the normal way, but before you start *add up* the number of digits after the decimal point in your original numbers: your answer must have that total number of digits after the decimal point. However you choose to do the long multiplication, 145 × 234 comes out as 33930. But 1.45 × 2.34 has a total of four decimal places, so the answer is 3.3930.

## Dividing decimals

With division, you want to get rid of the decimal point altogether. To divide 2.34 by 1.45, move the decimal point two places to the right in both cases, and divide 234 by 145 in the normal way. The answer is (approximately) 1.61, and if you use a calculator to divide 2.34 by 1.45, you'll prove to yourself that this method works.

It's worth noting that, just as you can add zeros to the left of a whole number and not change the value (001 is the same as 1), so you can do the same to the right of decimals: 1.50 is the same as 1.5, because that 0 is telling us that there are no hundredths to be taken into consideration.

This may seem an unnecessary piece of information, but it's handy when you come to convert decimals to ...

## Percentages

Percentages (usually written %) indicate a fraction of a hundred. Thus a half is 50%, because 50 is half of 100. A quarter is 25%, because 25 is a quarter of 100, and so on. This is where that bit about adding zeros to decimals comes in. Two numbers after a decimal point ('two decimal places') are the equivalent of hundredths, and therefore also of percentages:

0.50 = $^{50}/_{100}$, which cancels down to $^1/_2$ (divide the top and the bottom by the same number and it retains the same value, remember?). It also equals 50%.

0.25 = $^{25}/_{100}$ = $^1/_4$ = 25%

0.40 = $^{40}/_{100}$ = $^2/_5$ = 40%

## Discounts

In real life, it has to be said, we don't have much to do with fractions and decimals, but percentages are a handy tool whenever you are shopping during a sale. A discount off the original price is almost always expressed as a percentage, so it's useful to be able to do a quick sum in your head and work out what you are going to save. Probably the easiest way to do this is to convert the percentage to a fraction: 20% = $^{20}/_{100}$ = $^1/_5$, for example, and then do the multiplication sum described on page 38. So 20% off a £30 sweater is:

$$^1/_5 \times {^{30}/_1} = {^{30}/_5}$$

Divide 5 into 30 and you come up with a discount of £6. Deduct this from £30 and you are left with a sale price of £24. Bargain. Buy two while you're there.

It's also worth being able to approximate if the exact sum is too difficult. Say the discount is 35% off a £35 sweater. We may be able to convert $^{35}/_{100}$ to $^7/_{20}$, but not all of us can do

$$^7/_{20} \times {^{35}/_1}$$

in our heads. If we know that 33% is $^1/_3$, we can try that instead:

$$\tfrac{1}{3} \times {}^{35}\!/_1 = {}^{35}\!/_3$$

${}^{35}\!/_3$ doesn't divide equally, but ${}^{36}\!/_3$ does, to give £12. Deduct that from £35 and you have £23. It's not entirely accurate (the real answer is £22.75), but it's close enough for you to decide whether or not it is within your budget.

## Splitting the bill

Here's another instance where this sort of calculation comes in handy. There are five of you having dinner: two couples and a single. Each of the two husbands is paying for his wife (sexist, maybe, but it's what happened last time I conducted this experiment). The total bill is a convenient £150. You're dividing it equally, so in theory each individual is paying ⅕; in practice each husband is paying ⅖. To calculate ⅕, you divide by 5, which is £30. (If you find dividing by 5 difficult, just double the figure and divide by 10. In this case, that gives £300 divided by 10, which is £30.) To calculate ⅖, double that: £60. So the single person pays £30, the couples £60 each. To check, add the three figures together: £30 + £60 + £60 = £150, and you know you have it right.

Wait a minute, though. Service wasn't included. 10% is easy: we know that is the same as ¹⁄₁₀, and we know that £150 divided by 10 is £15, which is £3 per head or £6 per couple. (If you can't do that in your head, make sure that your mobile has a calculator function and carry it with you at all times.) But perhaps 10% is a bit mean: let's make it 12½%.

If you know that 50% is a half and 25% is a quarter, you should be able to work out that 12½% (half of 25) is an eighth. So to calculate 12½% of £150, you divide it by 8:

8 goes into 15 once, with 7 left over. Carry the 7 and divide 8 into 70 (this is where those times tables come in). With any luck, you remember that 8 × 8 is 64 and/or that 8 × 9 is 72. Either will help you here. 8 goes into 70 eight times, with 6 left over. Or, 8 doesn't quite go into 70 nine times.

Either way, the answer is almost £19. So a 12½% tip on a bill of £150 is almost £19. Most people would say it was too much bother to divide this evenly into 5, so round it up to £20 and pay £4 each, £8 per couple.

Another scenario: the bill is still £150, service included this time, but the single person is celebrating a pay rise and is going to pay for the wine. Let's say that costs £30. Deduct £30 from £150 and you are left with £120. That is the portion of the bill to be shared between the five people: £24 each. The two couples pay £48 each (2 × £24), a total of £96 (2 × £48). The single person pays £24, plus the £30 for the wine, £54 in total. Double check by adding the £54 to the £96 and you have the correct total: £150.

Whether you find this complicated or completely self-evident, make it a rule never to go out for dinner with people who say that they should pay less because they didn't have a starter or drank only mineral water. Not only do they complicate the sums, they are also too boring for words.

## THE LAW OF AVERAGES

An average – otherwise known as an **arithmetic mean** – is what you get when you add up a group of numbers and divide the result by the number of numbers involved.

The mean of $1 + 2 + 3 + 4 + 5$ is the total of those five numbers, 15, divided by 5 – in other words, 3. If you looked at our restaurant bill (see pages 42–3) from a different angle, you would find that the average expenditure for those five people was £30: £150 divided by 5.

School reports used to give an average mark for each subject, so that you could see how well your child was doing. Imagine, improbably, that there were fifteen children in the class and that they scored the following marks out of a hundred:

45, 47, 51, 54, 57, 63, 66, 67, 68, 69, 69, 73, 74, 77, 80

Those add up to 960; divide by 15 and you have an average of 64. You'll notice that no child actually scored 64%, but that doesn't stop it being the average.

### Median

Not to be confused with the mean is the **median**, which is simply the middle number in a sequence (provided that sequence is arranged in numerical order, of course). Take the marks given above and cross off the first one and the last one, then second and the second last and so on until you are left with the one in the middle, which is 67.

If the sequence has an even number of figures in it, the median is the average of the two middle figures (or, if you prefer, the mid-point between them). Let's take the lowest-scoring child out of our class above; we're left with fourteen students whose marks are:

47, 51, 54, 57, 63, 66, 67, 68, 69, 69, 73, 74, 77, 80

This adds up to 915, which divided by 14 gives a mean of 65.4 – a bit higher than before, as you would expect as you have taken out the lowest score. To find the median, cross out the end ones as before. This time you are left with two numbers rather than one – 67 and 68 – and a median of 67.5.

## Mode

This is simply the most commonly occurring number in any set of data. In the list above the only duplicated mark is 69, so that is the mode. If one of those children had scored 70, there would have been no duplication and therefore no mode. This may not seem very important when it comes to exam marks, but it matters in probability and statistics. Or so I am told.

## PRIME NUMBERS

A prime number is a whole positive number that cannot be divided by anything but itself and 1 to leave a whole number.

Huh?

OK, to start with, remember that a positive number is any number greater than zero (see page 35) and a whole number is one that doesn't have fractions or other bits and pieces attached: 1, 2, 3 are whole numbers; $1\frac{1}{2}$ and 2.5 are not.

Now, take the number 4. You can divide it by itself $(4 \div 4 = 1)$ and by 1 $(4 \div 1 = 4)$. You can also divide it by 2 $(4 \div 2 = 2)$. So it isn't prime.

The number 7 on the other hand – divide it by itself ($7 \div 7 = 1$), or by 1 ($7 \div 1 = 7$), fine. But try dividing it by anything else (2, 3, 4, 5) and you get 1 plus a bit left over. Therefore 7 is a prime number. The primes below 50 are 2, 3, 5, 7, 11, 13, 17, 19, 23, 29, 31, 37, 41, 43 and 47. Primes become fewer as you go higher because there are more numbers than might divide into them: there are fifteen primes below 50, but only another ten below 100.

And we care about this because ...? Well, frankly, unless we are mathematicians, for the most part we don't care at all. It's part of numbers theory, which to mathematicians is an end in itself. Or perhaps just a game that has no end. There are, however, two types of being who are not mathematicians and to whom prime numbers are important:

- Code-makers: large prime numbers (and computers have generated primes with more than 2 million digits) are apparently very useful for concocting unbreakable codes.

- Cicadas: if an animal has a life cycle of, say, four years, its predators can adapt their own life cycle to suit. Say the predator produces young every two years, it will, over time, learn to have more babies in the years when the prey species is abundant, and fewer when it is not. So one in every two predator life cycles hits the jackpot. Bad news for the prey. But if the prey species has a life cycle that is a prime number of years, predators find it much more difficult to adjust. There are some cicada species whose lives operate on a thirteen- or seventeen-year cycle, leading their predators to say, 'The hell with it. Let's go and eat something else.' Which, if you are a cicada, is a result.

## TAKING AN INTEREST

When you have money in the bank, they pay you interest. If you take out a mortgage, you pay back the money – with interest. Interest is calculated as a percentage of the **principal** – the sum of money invested or loaned – and it can be worked out in one of two ways.

### Simple interest

This means that you pay or are paid a certain sum at a certain time – once a month, once a year, etc. – and it makes no difference to the principal. Say you have invested £1000 and you are paid 5% interest a year. Your annual earnings will be £50, which is 5% of £1000 (see page 40 if you don't know why), for as long as the arrangement lasts. And that is all there is to it, which is why it is called simple.

### Compound interest

With **compound interest**, however, the interest payments are *added* to the principal, so that you earn interest on the interest.

To use the same example, after the first year, you receive your first interest payment of £50, making your principal up to £1050. The following year your interest is not £50, but £52.50, which is 5% of £1050. Your principal is now £1050

+ £52.50, or £1102.50. The following year your interest is £55.125, which is 5% of £1102.50.

## Doing the sums

**Simple interest** is calculated by the formula:

$$I = PRT$$

That is: interest = principal × rate × time

To get the final amount after all the interest has been paid, add the interest to the principal. To continue with our example, say your £1000 was invested for five years:

> $I = £1000 \times 0.05$ (5% converted to a decimal) × 5 (years) = £250. Add that to the principal and you have £1250 at the end of your five years.

**Compound** interest is calculated by the formula:

$$M = P \times (1 + i)^n$$

where M is the final amount (principal + interest), P is the principal, i is the rate of interest and n is the number of years.

So, in our example:

$$M = 1000 \times (1 + 0.05)^5$$

Following the BIDMAS principle outlined on page 36, we add the numbers in the bracket first and then deal with the power of 5, to give:

$$1.05 \times 1.05 \times 1.05 \times 1.05 \times 1.05 = 1.276$$

Multiply by 1000 and you have £1276, a whole £26 more than you earned with simple interest. This may not sound like a lot, but turn the principal into £200,000 and the length of time into twenty-five years and you will see why the interest payments on your mortgage end up being so huge.

## SQUARES AND SQUARE ROOTS

Finding the **square** of a number is fundamental to calculating area and volume, but it is perfectly straightforward: the square of any number is that number multiplied by itself:

$$4 \times 4 = 16$$
$$11 \times 11 = 121$$

so 16 is the square of 4 (written as $4^2$ and called 'four squared') and 121 is the square of 11.

When calculating volumes you need to take this one stage further and find a **cube**, which is the same number multiplied by itself three times:

$$4 \times 4 \times 4 = 64$$
$$11 \times 11 \times 11 = 1331$$

So 64 is 4 cubed ($4^3$) and 1331 is 11 cubed ($11^3$). If you want to go further (as when working out compound interest, see opposite), you can calculate the fourth, fifth and nth **power**, as these numbers are called, where n can be as large a number as you care to imagine.

The **square root**, represented by the sign ×, is the reverse of this process. From the above examples we know that 4 is the square root of 16 (×16) and 11 is the square root of 121

($\sqrt{121}$). Most calculators offer a square root function for more complicated sums. You can have cube roots, fourth roots and nth roots, too, but you won't often need them in real life.

A pedant might remark at this point that $4 \times 4 \times 4$ is actually four multiplied by itself only twice: there are two multiplication signs. True, but mathematical convention adds up the number of *numbers*, not the number of *functions*. There is no argument about $4 \times 4 \times 4$ being 'four to the power of three' or '$4^3$', so it is frankly just easier to say that this also means it is multiplied by itself three times.

## GEOMETRY

This is the branch of maths that concerns measuring things: working out angles between two lines, calculating areas and volumes. At school, if you remember, a lot of it was to do with triangles and the theorem put forward by a Greek mathematician called Pythagoras that the square on the hypotenuse equalled the sum of the square on the other two sides.

I feel another 'Huh?' moment coming on. Back to the beginning.

Where two lines meet, they form what is called an **angle** and its size is measured in **degrees**. 360° make up a circle, the angle along a straight line is 180° and a right angle (where one line is perpendicular to another) is 90°.

The total of the three angles of a triangle is also 180°, no matter how large or small each individual angle is. But if one of the angles is a right angle, the side opposite it – which is by definition the longest side – is called the hypotenuse, and this is where Pythagoras' theorem comes in:

The formula is $a^2 + b^2 = c^2$

where c is the hypotenuse and a and b are the other two sides. In a triangle whose sides are 3 cm, 4 cm and 5 cm and remembering to do multiplication before addition (see page 36), we can calculate quite easily that:

$$3 \times 3 + 4 \times 4 = 5 \times 5$$
or $$9 + 16 = 25$$

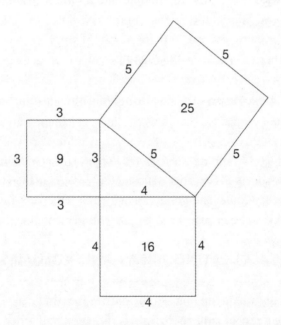

It works for much more complicated sums than that too. Mathematicians love Pythagoras' theorem because it is the basis of trigonometry, a branch of mathematics that can be used to calculate the height of trees and of mountains, to help architects produce buildings that can sway in the wind without falling down, to work out how far away the stars are and myriad other important things. But it also has uses closer to home: assuming you know the length of side a and side b, you can use Pythagoras to work out the length of the hypotenuse – which might tell you how much fencing you needed in a certain part of the garden, or whether you would save time driving diagonally cross-country rather than, say, east along one motorway then north along another.

Let's turn the driving example into a sum. It's 60 km east until you hit the northbound motorway, then 100 km north to your journey's end. 160 km in total if you take that route. But there's a decent-looking A road running diagonally north-east. That A road is the hypotenuse (c), and the 60- and 100-km motorways are sides a and b in our equation.

$$60^2 + 100^2 = 3600 + 10000 = 13600$$

So $c^2$ is 13,600 and, using a calculator, we find that its square root is 116.6. That's substantially less than the 160-km motorway route, and going this way may save you time and petrol if you can bear the grief you will get from the satnav.

## CALCULATING AREAS AND VOLUMES

The only way to do this is to memorize the formulae.

The **area of any rectangle** is its height multiplied by its breadth. If it is a square these two numbers will be the same.

The **area of a triangle** is half its base multiplied by its height. The height is always perpendicular to the base: with a non-right-angled triangle, you might have to draw a line outside the triangle itself to measure it.

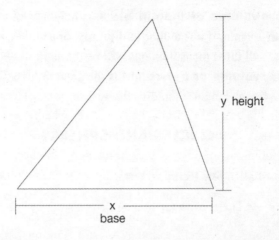

If you need to calculate the **area of a more complex shape** where no circles are involved, you can generally divide it into triangles and rectangles, calculate each individually and add them together. Say you are painting an attic bedroom with a sloping roof and want to calculate the surface area of each wall so that you know how much paint to buy:

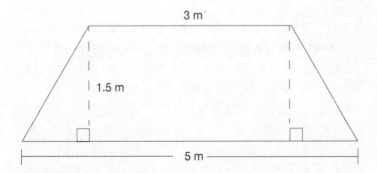

This awkward-looking area can be divided neatly into a rectangle and a triangle: problem solved.

The **volume of a solid block** is height by breadth by depth – again, if it is a cube (a dice, say, or a child's building block) all three measurements will be the same.

The **volume of a pyramid** is the area of the base multiplied by the height, then divided by three.

## CIRCLES AND SPHERES

First of all, a few technical terms:

- The **diameter** of a circle is a straight line through the middle.

- Half of this – a straight line from the central point to the outer ring – is the **radius**.

- The **circumference** is what in a straight-lined object is called the perimeter: the measurement round the outside.

### Pi

To calculate anything to do with circles and spheres, we need to introduce **pi**. Pi, pronounced 'pie' and usually written as the Greek letter $\pi$, represents the ratio – the relationship, if you prefer – between the diameter and the circumference of a circle. It's what scientists call a constant, which means, reasonably enough, that it never changes. Trying to calculate its exact value has kept mathematicians off the streets for many centuries and will continue to do so for many centuries to come; for our purposes it is enough to know that it is about 3.142 or $3\frac{1}{7}$ ($^{22}/_7$). (Don't forget you can refer back to Decimals on page 39 for help.)

The formula for calculating the **circumference of a circle** is πd or 2πr, where d = diameter and r = radius. Thus a circle that is 7 cm in diameter has a circumference of:

$$7 \times {}^{22}/_7 = 22 \text{ cm}$$

The **area of a circle** is πr². The same circle, 7 cm in diameter, has a radius of 3.5 cm, so its area is:

$$3.5 \times 3.5 \times 3.142 = 38.5 \text{ sq. cm}$$

Or, if you would rather do it in fractions:

$$3\frac{1}{2} \times 3\frac{1}{2} \times 3\frac{1}{7}$$

This converts to:

$$^7/_2 \times {}^7/_2 \times {}^{22}/_7$$

As we saw on page 38, the way to multiply fractions is to multiply the numerators together and then multiply the denominators together. This gives $^{1078}/_{28}$, which cancels down to $38\frac{1}{2}$.

Want to pave a circular area in the middle of the lawn and put a birdbath on it? This is the sum you need to do.

Three other formulae that, you never know, may come in handy one day:

- The **volume of a sphere** is $^4/_3\pi r^3$.

- The **volume of a cylinder** is its height multiplied by the area of its base, which of course is a circle. Thus the formula is $h \times \pi r^2$.

- A **cone** is effectively a pyramid with a circular base, so the formula is $(h \times \pi r^2) \div 3$.

## ALGEBRA

As in the $a^2 + b^2 = c^2$ of Pythagoras' theorem, on page 51, algebra uses letters instead of numbers. This enables you to solve a problem when you know the value of some but not all of a set of numbers, but know that they have a constant relationship to one another.

The most obvious example is, how long will it take you to drive from A to B? If we call distance d, speed s and time t, we can express this as an **equation**:

$$t = d \div s$$

You know the distance (say 160 km). You know the speed you will be travelling (an average of 40 kph). So you can simply divide 160 by 40 and come up with the answer: 4 hours.

Say, however, that you know the time and the speed, but want to calculate the distance. The rule with any equation is that whatever you do to the left-hand side, you must do exactly the same to the right-hand side – then it still works. If we take this equation and multiply each side by s, we come up with:

$$t \times s = d \div s \times s$$

On the right-hand side, multiplying by s and dividing by s cancel each other out, so we can reduce this to:

$$t \times s = d$$

Thus in our example, we can calculate that:

$$4 \text{ hours (t)} \times 40 \text{ kph (s)} = 160 \text{ km travelled (d)}$$

and so on.

A more complicated example: a sales price of £33 includes VAT (or sales tax or any other add-on of that sort) and you need to know how much tax you are paying. At the time of writing, the standard rate of VAT in the UK is 20%, so let's use that. But the principle is the same whether it is 5%, 50% or anything in between.

Tax is added to a basic or **net** price to produce a **gross** price, which is generally what the customer pays. The common mistake in this sum is to treat the sales price as 100%, when it should be 120%. Or, to express is as an equation:

net price (n, 100%) + tax (t, 20%) = gross price (g, 120%)

As with the speed/distance/time sum above, we know the values of two of the three elements in our equation and can use them to calculate the third. We know that g = £33. We also know that t is 20%, or $\frac{1}{5}$, of n. Put that another way, n is 5 times t. Let's put that information into our equation:

$$n + t = £33$$

becomes

$$5t + t = £33$$

In other words:

$$6t = £33$$

Now, remembering that if we make the same change to either side of the equation it still works, we divide both sides by 6 and come up with:

$$t = £33 \div 6 = £5.50$$

Thus, if you are registered for VAT, you can claim £5.50 back from the tax authorities. Keep that receipt.

## PROBABILITY

Here we come to the vital area that calculates how likely you are to win the lottery (not very) or throw a 7 with two ordinary dice (better than average). It is also the branch of maths that enables an insurance company to calculate premiums: where you live, how old you are, what sort of car you drive and what your previous driving record is are all factors that weigh in the probability of your having an accident or having your car stolen.

Probability is calculated on a scale of – wait for it – 0 to 1. Yes, all the variations from the stereotypical careful lady owner in a small town to the equally stereotypical inner-city boy racer in an ancient Ford are encompassed in that tiny range. Put simply, anything that is impossible ranks as 0, anything that is certain is 1, and anything that is possible, however likely or unlikely it may be, falls in between.

Take a conventional six-sided dice. The chance of rolling an 8 with a single throw is 0 (it can't be done), the chance of rolling any one of 1, 2, 3, 4, 5 and 6 is 1 (whatever happens, one of these is going to turn up). But the chance of rolling a specific number – say 3 – is one in six: $\frac{1}{6}$. The chance of *not* rolling a 3 is $\frac{5}{6}$, because there are five other numbers that have an equal chance of turning up.

These probabilities are also often expressed as percentages, particularly when the odds are even, as it were. When you toss a coin there are only two possible outcomes – heads or tails – and each is as likely as the other. Thus there is a 50% (or 50–50) chance that the coin will come down heads, and an equally 50% chance that it will be tails.

It's when you try to predict a sequence of events that calculating odds becomes more complicated. Any time you toss a coin, there is a 50% chance of a head. But the chances of your throwing four heads in a row are smaller: obviously, if you throw a tail first time, you're scuppered. So you begin with a 50% (or $\frac{1}{2}$) chance of throwing a head, and follow it by a 50% chance of throwing a second head and so on. You can calculate the odds by multiplying each throw together:

$$\frac{1}{2} \times \frac{1}{2} \times \frac{1}{2} \times \frac{1}{2} = \frac{1}{16}$$

Under normal circumstances, you have only a 1 in 16 chance (a bit over 6%) of turning up four heads in a row.

Try the same with dice: what are the chances of throwing three 3s in a row? Well, there is a one in six chance of getting a 3 at any given throw, so multiply $\frac{1}{6} \times \frac{1}{6} \times \frac{1}{6}$ and you find that you have 1 chance in 216, or a little under 0.5%.

What the insurance people do is slightly more complicated, but it boils down to:

careful lady owner + garage + no accidents in ten years

is a better bet than

just passed his test + parks on the street + can't be trusted not to show off to his mates.

As the saying goes, you do the maths.

# SCIENCE

If you weren't one of those to whom science came naturally, you may have felt that all that theory, all those equations and all those laws about gases you learnt at school were just a bit pointless. So, although I've divided this chapter into biology, chemistry and physics in the conventional way, I've tackled each topic from the point of view of a practical, daily-life sort of issue. With any luck, therefore, it'll give you answers to some of the questions that all too often began with 'Who gives a \*\*\*\* about ...?'

## BIOLOGY

Although your days of dissecting frogs are probably a distant memory, biology still has its uses. This section touches on ecology, genetics, amino acids, bacteria and viruses and plant cell biology – surely enough to reignite some of that long-dormant interest.

### Will your children have blue eyes or brown?

OK, not an entirely everyday question, but nonetheless one that a lot of people speculate about. Eye colour is dictated by **genes**. Each gene is a length of DNA which carries the code required to produce a specific protein and therefore to determine eye colour, hair colour and other aspects of physical appearance (not to mention gender, intelligence, a tendency to certain diseases and myriad other things).

Quantities of genes go together to form a **chromosome**. The normal human body contains forty-six chromosomes in twenty-three matching pairs; during reproduction the pairs from the mother split and half of them come together with half of those from the father, so that the offspring inherits a combination of the genes of both parents. Different versions of the same gene are called **alleles**.

At its simplest, the alleles are either **dominant** or **recessive**. With eye colour, a blue allele is generally recessive and brown dominant. This means that in order to produce blue eyes, a child must inherit two 'blue' alleles, one on each chromosome in the appropriate pair. If there was a combination of blue and brown, the brown would dominate.

So if both parents have blue eyes, there are only 'blue' elements present and the baby will have blue eyes.

However, a person with brown eyes may have two brown alleles, or they may have just one brown allele, plus a recessive blue allele. Say both parents are what is called **heterozygous** (they have two different alleles, a blue and a brown), the possible combinations for their children are:

blue from mother + blue from father = blue-eyed baby
blue from mother + brown from father = brown-eyed baby
brown from mother + blue from father = brown-eyed baby
brown from mother + brown from father = brown-eyed baby

Because brown eyes will appear wherever there is a brown allele, there is a one in four chance that these parents will produce a blue-eyed child but a two in three chance that a brown-eyed child will be carrying a recessive blue allele, which may then appear in a later generation.

If one parent is **homozygous** for brown eyes (that is, he or she is carrying two brown alleles) and the other parent is heterozygous, the baby will have brown eyes whatever happens. But again there is a one in two chance that it will be carrying the recessive blue gene.

## Why do certain foods make you sleepy?

This could be because they contain an amino acid called tryptophan, which is converted in the body into two hormones that cause sleepiness, serotonin and melatonin. Amino acids are the 'building blocks' of protein, but it is the action of carbohydrates that helps make tryptophan available to the brain; it is therefore the carbohydrate-heavy foods such as bread, pasta and potatoes that make us sleepy. Also a factor in the conversion of tryptophan is the mineral calcium, found in dairy products, oily fish and green vegetables, among other foods.

So, given that most people have a natural slump in activity in the early afternoon anyway (to do with body clocks rather than eating habits), it's best not to combine protein and carbohydrate at lunchtime if you need to work afterwards. For the same reason, a glass of milk (which is rich in both protein and carbohydrate) is much better at bedtime than tea or coffee, whose caffeine content gives a short-term kick.

And what about chocolate, I hear you cry? Well, forget all that stuff about blueberries and other alleged 'super foods' absorbing the free radicals that contribute so much to the ageing process. A website that is admittedly called Chocolate Necessities Inc. maintains that dark chocolate contains almost five and a half times as many ORACs ('oxygen radical absorbance capacity' units) as blueberries and nearly fifteen times as many as broccoli. (Hooray, shouts every schoolboy and no small number of grown men reading this.) Chocolate also boosts the level of serotonin, mentioned above, an action that is mimicked by many pharmaceutical anti-depressants. Bad news: the quantity of dark chocolate that is reckoned to be good for you is about 30 grams a day. Not enough to justify throwing the broccoli out altogether.

## Why do you have to take a full course of antibiotics, even though you're feeling better?

Because the bacteria that antibiotics combat are so darned clever, that's why. They adapt very quickly to changes in their environment; they also reproduce and mutate at an alarming rate. Antibiotics will kill some of them straight away, but not all of them, so if you stop taking the tablets the bacteria that were lurking in the background may well be able to build up a resistance to the antibiotic and infect you all over again. While the others die, these new, drug-resistant bacteria will *survive* – because they are *the fittest*. It is Darwin's theory of evolution operating inside your body in the space of a very few days. How scary is that?

By the way, colds are caused not by bacteria but by viruses, which don't take a blind bit of notice of antibiotics. That's why, if you go to your doctor with a cold, she'll tell you to go away and take paracetamol: nothing she can prescribe will be any more effective than the stuff you buy over the counter in the pharmacist's. So don't waste her time.

## Why does yeast make dough rise?

Yeast is a fungus, which means it is already a living organism, but it takes on a new lease of life, as it were, when you add warm water to it. It then feeds on carbohydrates, like the flour in bread dough and the sugar in beer, and produces carbon dioxide and alcohol. It is the slow release of carbon dioxide from the yeast that makes the dough rise. The dough is then baked at a sufficiently high temperature to kill off the alcohol, which is why you don't get plastered if you have an extra slice of toast in the morning.

Beer-making experts differentiate between top-fermenting yeasts (for lager) and bottom-fermenting ones (for ale), but that is sadly beyond the scope of this chapter.

## What's all the fuss about biodiversity and monocultures?

*Mono* is from the Greek for one (as in *monopoly*, *monogamy* and *monomaniac*). A **monoculture** is an area where only a single species grows – a plantation that focuses on one crop, for example. It tends to be man-made, doesn't generally occur when nature is left to her own devices and is broadly speaking a bad thing.

The opposite of a monoculture is **biodiversity** (*bio* comes from the Greek for life, and I'm not going to insult you by telling you what *diversity* means). This is a concept much extolled by environmentalists, because it means that lots of different plants grow side by side, supporting lots of insects, which in turn supply lots of foods for birds, etc., etc. Insects are often very specialized feeders, dependent on only one species of plant, so almost by definition a monoculture cannot support much life. Also, if it falls victim to a disease or a pest, it will be wiped out at a stroke, something that is much less likely to happen in a biodiverse environment. (You may have heard of an insect called phylloxera, which periodically ravages wine-growing areas across the world. Vineyards are, of course, an example of a monoculture that is a good thing, but even so they are vulnerable to this sort of attack.)

The point is, if we want the world to continue to house hummingbirds and orangutans, we need to save the rainforests (the supreme example of biodiversity) and not let them all be turned into palm-oil plantations.

On a smaller scale, organic gardeners are interested in diversity because it can be used to protect crops. Growing marigolds in the greenhouse, for example, will keep whitefly away from your tomatoes, because the insects appear not to like the smell. Growing sage near carrots repels carrot fly for the same reason. It's all part of the message that nature is meant to embrace a wide variety of stuff.

## Why should you snip the bases off the stems of cut flowers?

Aha! Plant cell biology in a vase.

**Xylem** and **phloem** form a plant's 'circulatory system'. Phloem carries mostly sugars (produced by photosynthesis) around the plant, while xylem carries water and minerals. One kind of xylem is better known as the wood in trees; it also enables softer-stemmed plants to stand upright. But it is its liquid-bearing ability that concerns us here.

Think of xylem as a collection of the sort of straws you drink through (but not the bendy kind they give you with cocktails – that would be too befuddling in all sorts of ways). If the bottom of the straw is in water, you suck up water. If not, you suck up air – which, if you are thirsty, is no use at all. Following the same broad principle, a cut plant out of water will form an air pocket at the end of the xylem, preventing water from getting through. So for best results, put the stems of your cut flowers into water and, cutting at an angle to expose more of the ends of the xylem, remove about 5 cm from the base of each.

Remember also that plants get their nutrients from their roots. If you cut flowers to put them in a vase, you are depriving them of their source of 'food': that's why florists supply little packets of nutrients for you to add to the water.

And, before we move on, did you have one of those flickers of vague recognition at the mention of photosynthesis a couple of paragraphs ago? Well, just to remind you, *photo* comes from the Greek for light and photosynthesis is the way in which plants process light to produce food for themselves. In addition to light and water, they need carbon dioxide from the atmosphere, to produce a reaction like this:

$$6CO_2 + 6H_2O \text{ (plus light energy from the sun)} \rightarrow$$
$$C_6H_{12}O_6 + 6O_2$$

You probably recognize $CO_2$ as carbon dioxide, $H_2O$ as water and $O_2$ as oxygen. That scary-looking compound $C_6H_{12}O_6$ isn't actually scary at all. It's glucose, the simplest form of sugar, which the plant uses to manufacture the more complex carbohydrates it needs for growth.

## CHEMISTRY

This really is going back to basics, talking about atoms and molecules – the tiniest particles into which things can be divided unless you know a very great deal of chemistry indeed. I've also taken chemistry out of the lab and put it into the kitchen and bathroom, just for good measure!

### Why does bubble bath disappear when you wash yourself with soap?

To answer this question we need to look at the difference between an atom and a molecule. An **atom** is defined as the smallest particle in an element that can take part in a chemical reaction: the fact that Ernest Rutherford managed to 'split' one in 1917 came as something of a surprise to the uninitiated, who didn't know this was possible. Anyway, an atom consists of a nucleus made up of neutral **neutrons** and positively charged **protons**, around which orbit negatively charged **electrons**. Under normal circumstances, an atom has the same number of protons as electrons, which balance each other so that the atom has no electrical charge. It is the movement of electrons – upsetting the balance by making an atom positive or negative – that causes a chemical reaction. An atom with an electric charge is called an **ion**.

Put two or more atoms together and you have a **molecule**. Combine an atom of nitrogen with three of hydrogen in the right conditions and you produce a molecule of ammonia ($NH_3$). You need three hydrogens because of a property that all atoms possess called **valency**, which means the number of atoms of hydrogen each displaces when forming a compound.

It stands to reason that hydrogen has a valency of one; nitrogen in this instance has a valency of three. Valency is a complicated subject because it can vary even within the same element, but the point here is that valencies need to 'match' in order for the atoms to react together to form a compound.

So if you add bubble bath to your bath water and then wash yourself with soap, the positively charged molecules present in bubble bath are cancelled out by the negative ones in soap, so the bubbles collapse. A lesson there, I feel: bubble bath is for relaxing in; it shouldn't be confused with getting clean.

## What's the difference between cake and bread?

While we're on the subject of the properties of molecules, and this one will really impress your dinner-party guests, let's look at the difference between cake and bread. Admit it, you've never thought about it, have you? Well, the answer is a simple, all-too-familiar, one-syllable word: fat. The flour generally used in cake- and bread-making contains proteins that absorb water. Add water to flour and it will form gluten, the stuff that makes bread dough sticky and elastic. *But*, add butter or margarine, as you do in most cakes, and the result is completely different. Fat does not dissolve in water, so it stops the proteins doing their thing. Hence, springy, chewy bread and soft, crumbly cake.

## Why does stale cake go hard and stale biscuits go soft?

Sticking with the subject of cake, have you ever wondered why stale cake and stale biscuits have such a different consistency from one another, despite the fact that they are made from much the same ingredients? It's to do with **osmosis**, the process by which water moves from an area of higher moisture to one of lower moisture. If you've followed the instructions correctly, cakes start off moist, so it is in the nature of things for the water to evaporate, making the cake drier and harder. Biscuits are baked to the point of dehydration – when they are fresh they are crisp and crunchy, but as time goes by they will absorb moisture from an atmosphere that is moister than they are.

And, reverting to the subject of whether or not something is soluble in water, if you are gasping over a hot curry, drink milk rather than water. Capsaicin, the ingredient of chilli that makes it hot, is soluble in fat (which even skimmed milk contains a little of) but not in water, so milk will be much more effective in cooling you down.

## Why is helium good in balloons?

With an atomic number of 2 and an atomic mass of 4.003, helium is the second lightest of all the elements (only hydrogen beats it). It is appreciably lighter than air, which is almost 80 per cent nitrogen (atomic number 7, atomic mass just over 14), so it floats on air for the same reason that a plastic bottle floats on water: it's lighter than the air or water it has displaced.

Buoyancy is a funny thing: scientists reckon that the planet Saturn, being made of gases, is so undense that if you put it in water it would float. Mind you, you would need a lot of water.

To get back to the point, helium's other advantage is that it is what is called an inert gas: it reacts with almost nothing.

This gives it a major advantage over hydrogen as a filler for balloons, because hydrogen is highly flammable and would ruin a birthday party if it got too close to the candles on the cake.

The reason that helium makes your voice squeaky is to do with the way your voice works. Normally, air passing over the vocal cords causes them to vibrate and this produces sound waves. Because helium is much less dense than air, sound waves travel through it more quickly, producing the Donald Duck noises familiar to anyone who has ever taken this particular route to being the life and soul of the party.

## Why does vinegar remove limescale from kettles?

Limescale is another name for calcium carbonate, which is formed by the calcium ions found in 'hard' water. Vinegar contains acetic acid. Part-filling a 'scaly' kettle with vinegar, then adding water and boiling it up produces a chemical reaction:

Calcium carbonate + acetic acid + water + heat →
hot water + carbon dioxide + calcium acetate

Calcium acetate is a salt that dissolves in water (calcium carbonate does not, which is why it builds up as a deposit). So once you have rinsed away all the vinegary residue, you can make a decent cup of tea again.

Mention of the word 'salt' brings us to the aspect of this that you probably learnt in chemistry: acids, bases and salts.

An **acid** is a compound that contains hydrogen ions; when an acid is dissolved in water, it gives off those hydrogen ions.

On the other hand, when you dissolve a **base** (also known, less accurately, as an alkali) in water it *receives* hydrogen ions. An ion, as we saw on page 68, is an atom with either a positive or a negative charge.

The result of this activity produces, among other things, a **salt**, which is usually a solid crystalline compound in which the positive ions from the base have replaced the hydrogen ions in the acid.

The chemical formula for calcium acetate is $Ca(C_2H_3O_2)_2$, which is more complicated than anything most of us learnt at school and is the reason I gave the equation on the previous page in words rather than symbols. But this sort of chemical reaction doesn't need to look intimidating. Say, for example, you added hydrochloric acid (HCl) to washing soda (sodium carbonate, $Na_2CO_3$), which is a base, the two compounds would simply swap components to give this equation:

$$2HCl + Na_2CO_3 \rightarrow 2NaCl + H_2CO_3$$

$H_2CO_3$ is the formula for carbonic acid, a weak acid that can also be formed by the reaction of carbon dioxide and water, and NaCl or sodium chloride is everyone's favourite salt – common table salt. Hydrochloric acid, on the other hand, is corrosive and unpleasant, so please don't try this at home.

## PHYSICS

It's more popular now than it's ever been, and for good reason – physics is a fascinating subject that gets to the bottom of why we're here and how we're made. This brief foray into how the eye absorbs colour, the laws of thermodynamics, electricity and light and sound waves will, I hope, give you some idea of why physics has been put back on the map.

## How can you tell if colours will clash?

Let's start with the colours of the spectrum, which you may well have learnt as Richard Of York Gave Battle In Vain – red, orange, yellow, green, blue, indigo and violet. All light that is naturally visible to the human eye falls into this spectrum –beyond it at one end is infra (below) red and at the other ultra (beyond) violet. Each colour has a different wavelength, red being the longest and violet the shortest. When these wavelengths strike an object, that object will absorb the ones that correspond to the pigments it contains and reflect the others. Thus the structure of a daffodil enables it to absorb every colour except yellow; it reflects the yellow and that is what we see.

We humans identify colours using light-sensitive cells known as cones in the retina at the back of the eye. (The retina also contains rods, which are important for peripheral and night vision, and ganglions, which detect slow changes in light that enable us to assess what time of day it is by looking out the window.) From the cones' point of view there are three primary colours – red, green and blue (the RGB of television and computer screens). Each cone responds to a colour range based around one of these colours. Put them together and they can detect subtle tones of yellow, mauve and peacock blue.

Isaac Newton (he's the one who discovered the spectrum – there was no end to the man's talents) didn't know about cones in the eye. He based his theory of colour on red, yellow and blue, on the basis that all the colours of the spectrum could be made from them. Modern painters and printers have moved away from this limited colour range, but in terms of wavelengths it still works. Two complementary colours will contain all three of Newton's primary colours, thus:

> red is complementary to green (blue + yellow)
> blue is complementary to orange (red + yellow)
> yellow is complementary to violet (red + blue)

Try staring at a certain colour for a minute, then shift your gaze to a white wall. You'll see an image of the complementary colour, because the colour receptors in your eyes will be tired of the colour you've been looking at and will compensate. If you've been looking at red, for example, you'll see green.

These complementary colours are the ones that are often described as clashing. Most people would say, for example, that red didn't 'go' with green, or blue with orange. Of course this takes no account of different shades or tones of colour, and you may want to wear or decorate in clashing colours to make a statement. Fine, but be aware that it will send a lot of people groping for their sunglasses.

You'll notice an absence of indigo in this discussion. Including indigo in the spectrum was another of Newton's ideas – because seven was a lucky number, because it made the 'Richard of York' mnemonic work? – but modern colour scientists tend to ignore it and lump it in with violet, so I have done the same.

And if you've noticed that there has been no mention of black or white, that's because, as far as our eyes are concerned, white is a reflection of all visible light, while black is total absorption or absence of light. Neither of them is a colour in the Newtonian sense.

## How do you keep your tea piping hot?

In order to answer this question we first need to look at **thermodynamics** – that is, the study of heat and its relationship with other forms of energy. Its laws state:

1)  The amount of energy in a closed system (one which is not influenced by external factors) is constant. It cannot be created or destroyed, although it can change from one form to another.

2)  In a closed system, heat will always spread out as evenly as it can, but it will not spontaneously move from a cold body to a hot one.

3)  When the temperature of a system is absolute zero (–273°C), its entropy will be zero. Entropy is the measure of 'disorder' in a system. A gas, whose particles float around all over the place, has more entropy than a liquid, which in turn is less orderly than a solid.

And, as I may have asked elsewhere in this book, we care about this because …?

Well, heat transfer is important in all sorts of everyday things such as heating a room or boiling a kettle. It occurs in one of three ways:

- conduction

- convection

- radiation

**Conduction** can occur in solids, liquids and gases and brings the Second Law into play: it involves a hot object coming into contact with a cold one and transferring its heat. Many metals are good conductors of heat – you don't have to leave a teaspoon in a cup of hot coffee for long to feel conduction in action.

**Convection** is confined to liquids and gases and is discussed in the Geography chapter with reference to winds (see page 141). It applies to convection ovens too. In either case, hot air rises, cold air rushes in to take its place, warms up and rises in its turn, and so *ad infinitum*. Adding hot water to a bath and thus heating the water that is already there but beginning to cool down is a crucial example of convection in action – crucial, at least, if you are in the bath and want to finish your chapter before you get out.

**Radiation** works in a different way, through infrared waves. Because of this, it is the only one of the three methods that can conduct heat in a vacuum. All matter emits and absorbs this form of heat/energy, so radiation is responsible for all manner of things from the warmth of the sun's rays to the way a toaster turns bread into toast.

Heat is lost through the surface of a hot object, and there are various ways in which heat loss can be reduced. A poor conductor of heat is called an insulator, like that fluffy stuff you put in the loft to stop heat escaping through the roof. Shiny surfaces don't emit radiation as well as matt ones do, which is why marathon runners are wrapped in foil blankets at the end of a race – the shiny foil minimizes the loss of body heat.

If you aren't planning on running a marathon in the immediate future, you may be more interested in keeping a mug of coffee warm while you empty the washing machine or check your emails. Choice of mug material and shape is the key here. Earthenware and glass are better insulators than metal and thick is better than thin – so delicate bone china isn't much good either. Because heat is lost through the surface, a tall thin mug is better than a low wide one. Shame that so many of those tall thin ones are made of delicate bone china.

One other thing on the subject of heat: have you ever wondered why you are always told to stir things after half the cooking time in the microwave? It's because of the risk of a phenomenon called **superheating**, when a liquid is heated to above its boiling point without appearing to boil. Surface tension prevents the bubbles that normally indicate boiling from forming and the heating continues. Then when you move the container it may boil very rapidly and spray scalding water or steam over you. Stirring breaks the surface tension and reduces the risk of this happening; so does putting a wooden spoon or other poor conductor of heat into the container. The third precaution is to use a container that isn't brand new and smooth-sided: pits and scratches on the inside surface should allow bubbles to form and avoid that build-up of tension.

## Do long electric cables deliver less power than shorter ones?

This is to do with resistance, so before we attempt to answer the question, let's define some familiar terms in the electricity world.

The amount of electric **current** flowing through a cable – or any other conductive material – at any given time is measured in **amps** (short for amperes). Electricity flows from an area of high negative charge to an area of low negative charge; the difference between these two areas is known as the **potential difference** and is measured in **volts**. Multiply current by potential difference (amps by volts) and the answer is **power**, which is measured in **watts**.

Anything that impedes the flow of electricity is **resistance**, measured in **ohms**. To calculate resistance, divide the voltage by the current: what it boils down to is that if a current meets resistance, it needs more voltage (oomph, if you prefer) to get through. Even a really good conductor of electricity, such as silver, gives *some* resistance to electricity flow, so the answer to our original question is yes: a long cable will contain more resistance (and therefore carry less power) than a short one. For domestic purposes, however, this is likely to be negligible, so don't feel you have to move the furniture around to avoid using an extension cable.

Length is a much more important factor when it comes to USB cables. For complicated reasons connected with the fact that it is conveying primarily information rather than power, a standard-issue USB cable cannot be more than 5 metres long. Unless you want to get into specialist equipment, this is an occasion when you do need to move the furniture – or at least take the laptop nearer to the power point.

## Why do different countries have different voltages?

Simply because they have different regulations about how electricity is transported from source to consumer. The norm in the US is 110 volts, less than half the 230 that is standard in the EU and the 240 prevalent in the UK. The lower the voltage, the less powerfully the current will flow, as any Brit who has ever waited for a kettle to boil in the US will have noticed. Appliances such as kettles are normally designed to tolerate some variation in voltage, so a British one won't blow a fuse if you plug it into a French socket. An American one will, though. The sort of adaptor you buy when you go on holiday may simply allow you to fit a three-point plug into a two-point socket; a transformer will also cope with the change in voltage.

## What does the wattage of a light bulb mean?

It's a way of measuring how much power the bulb consumes. A sixty-watt bulb consumes roughly sixty watts an hour; it is therefore 40 per cent cheaper to run than a hundred-watt bulb. Electricity bills are based on the number of kilowatt-hours (*kilo* = 1,000) you have consumed: it will take ten hours for a hundred-watt bulb to use up a kilowatt-hour of electricity and sixteen and two-thirds hours for a sixty-watt bulb to do the same.

A hundred-watt bulb probably gives out more light than a sixty-watt bulb, but the real key to light intensity is the number of lumens. The lumen is the standard measurement of luminous flux, which is taking us into waters too deep for this chapter (and waters are, of course, a dangerous place to go when dealing with electricity). Just take my word for it: the more lumens, the brighter the light.

## Should you turn the light off when you leave a room?

There is a surprising number of factors to consider here. When you switch a light on, it uses more electrical energy than it does when it is running, but only the equivalent of a few seconds. So turn it off. But doing this too often with a low-energy fluorescent bulb will shorten its lifespan. So leave it on. But the electricity it consumes if you leave it on costs more than a replacement bulb. So turn it off. But then you have to throw the bulb away and add to landfill, compromising your decision to buy an energy-efficient bulb in the first place. You're sorry you asked, aren't you?

## How far away is a thunderstorm?

The speed of light is very close to 300,000 km per second. This means that if you were standing on the moon, you would see a flash of lightning on earth in little more than a second. Let's say 'instantly', as we are among friends.

Sound travels rather more slowly: at 340 metres a second. If you were standing 340 metres away from a storm, the sound would reach you a second after you saw the lightning. (If you were standing on the moon it would take over twelve days.) Count the number of seconds between seeing the lightning and hearing the thunder, multiply the answer by 340 and the result will be the number of metres you are away from the storm. This sum is much easier if you are lucky enough to think in miles: just divide the number of seconds by five.

According to the American National Weather Service, there are 1,800 storms going on around the world at any given moment – 16 million a year. Even so, the average American has only a one in 10,000 chance of being struck by lightning during his or her lifetime. The service still warns us all to stay indoors during a storm and not to consider a tent, a greenhouse or a golf buggy a safe form of shelter.

# HISTORY

Where to start? What to put in and what to leave out? When the subject is as vast as world history, the answers to those questions have to be selective. This chapter, therefore, is primarily a timeline of some key events of the last 600 years, with occasional deviations to expand on topics where the theme of 'Oh yes, remind me – what was that about?' seems most pertinent.

**1453** Constantinople, which has been in Christian hands, falls to the Turks; it becomes the capital of the Muslim Ottoman Empire. Refugee Christian scholars bring their knowledge into Western Europe, fuelling the Renaissance (see opposite).

**1455** Johannes Gutenberg's Bible, the first book produced using movable type, is completed: for the first time books can be mass-produced and the spread of information is taken out of the control of the Church. Many people regard this as the single most important event in history.

**1472** The Portuguese explorer Lopo Gonçalves crosses the equator and discovers the Southern Hemisphere.

**1485** The Wars of the Roses end when Richard III is defeated and killed at the Battle of Bosworth. Henry Tudor becomes Henry VII, the first monarch of the Tudor dynasty.

## The Renaissance

The name means 'rebirth' and it's used to refer to the rebirth of interest in all things Greek and Roman – art, literature, architecture, philosophy – which began in Italy as early as the twelfth century and spread across Europe over the next 400 years. Along with it came a flowering of humanist ideas that emphasized the intellectual, scientific and philosophical importance of Man.

Many of the great names of the Renaissance had more than one talent: Leonardo da Vinci (painter, designer, engineer, student of anatomy and mirror-writing), Michelangelo (painter, sculptor and poet), Brunelleschi (architect, sculptor and goldsmith), Vasari (architect, painter and art historian) and many more. Although all these people were Italian, the label Renaissance may also be attached to the great Dutch humanist scholar Erasmus, the German theologian Martin Luther (see **The Reformation** on page 85), the English writers of the Elizabethan period, including Shakespeare, Christopher Marlowe and Edmund Spenser, and the French poets Joachim du Bellay and Pierre de Ronsard.

Hand in hand with humanist thought came advances in science and technology: there was Gutenberg (see **1455**, opposite), explorers who wanted to show that the earth was round and the Polish astronomer Nicolaus Copernicus, one of the first to put forward the heretical suggestion that the earth moved round the sun: all 'Renaissance men'.

**1488** The Portuguese explorer Bartolomeu Dias rounds the Cape of Good Hope.

### The Age of Exploration

Intrepid Europeans set out to discover and lay claim to the rest of the world, not to mention establishing a slave trade that would last over 300 years. In 1492 'Columbus sails the ocean blue' and claims some of the Caribbean islands for Spain (though he was himself Italian), marking the beginning of an extended period of Spanish colonization of southern and Central America. Other 'big names' of the period include John Cabot, the first European to make landfall in North America since the Vikings (1497), the Portuguese Vasco da Gama, who leads the first voyage from Europe to India (1498) and the Italian Amerigo Vespucci, who, under the service of the King of Portugal, makes several voyages to the Americas (1499–1502) and claims to be the first to sight South America.

**1492** The Reconquista ('Reconquest') of Spain is completed under the 'Catholic monarchs' Ferdinand and Isabella. The Moors are expelled from Granada; Spain is united as a Christian country. Ferdinand has established the Spanish Inquisition (didn't expect that, did you?) with a remit to combat heresy, monitor converted Jews and Muslims, suppress witchcraft and ban books he doesn't want people to read. This cheery organization, whose methods include torture and burning at the stake, is not officially abolished until well into the nineteenth century.

**1494** Spain and Portugal sign the Treaty of Tordesillas, agreeing to divide the world outside of Europe between them.

## The Reformation

The Reformation of the Christian Church may be said to begin when in 1517 German theologian Martin Luther protests against the selling of 'indulgences' – pardons for sins that are supposed to be earned through repentance and absolution. Before this time, the entire Western Christian Church has been Catholic (following the Great Schism of 1054, which saw the Catholic Church divide into Eastern [orthodox] and Western Churches); now various categories of 'Protestants' come into being. In England this will cause great conflict over the Tudor royal succession – Henry VIII's Protestant son, Edward VI, tries to ensure that, in the absence of male heirs, his Catholic half-sister Mary will not become queen. No luck: his chosen successor, Lady Jane Grey, is beheaded after a reign of nine days. In France, the growing political power of the Huguenots (followers of the second great Protestant reformer, John Calvin) leads to the Wars of Religion (off and on between 1562 and 1598); several thousand leading Huguenots are massacred around the feast day of St Bartholomew (24 August) 1572.

**1519** The Spanish king becomes the Holy Roman Emperor Charles V and now rules much of Europe and the New World.

**1520** Under the Spanish flag, the Portuguese explorer Ferdinand Magellan discovers a route to circumnavigate the globe. He himself is killed in the Philippines but his ships go on to complete the journey.

**1520** Suleiman the Magnificent becomes the tenth Sultan of the (Turkish) Ottoman Empire and presides over the height of the empire's power and prestige.

**1520** The Spanish soldier Hernán Cortés seizes Mexico. He captures Tenochtitlán, the capital of the Aztec Empire, the following year.

**1526** The Mughal Empire, descended from the Mongol conquests of the thirteenth century, begins its rule of India.

**1533** The Grand Prince of Moscow, Ivan the Terrible, becomes the first ruler to be crowned Tsar.

**1534** France begins its colonization of North America ('New France') when the French explorer Jacques Cartier claims Canada.

**1534** The Society of Jesus, also known as the Jesuits, the Catholic missionary order of the Counter-Reformation, is established.

**1545–63** The Council of Trent aims to strengthen the Catholic Church in its resistance to Protestantism.

**1548** The Haijin laws issued by the Ming government in China curb foreign trade.

**1556** Akbar the Great succeeds to the throne of the Mughal Empire and presides over its 'Classic Period'.

**1558** Calais, which for two centuries has been part of the Kingdom of England, is taken by the French.

**1559** The Italian Wars culminate in the end of the Italian city-states (although Savoy and Venice remain independent states); Milan, Naples and Sicily are annexed to Spain.

**1568** The Eighty Years' War breaks out when the Seventeen Provinces of the Low Countries revolt against their ruler, Philip II of Spain.

**1568** The end of the 'Warring States Period' sees the unification of Japan.

**1571** The Holy League – an alliance of most of the Catholic states bordering the Mediterranean – is victorious against the Ottomans at the sea battle of Lepanto.

**1572** The last Inca stronghold in Peru is conquered by the Spanish.

**1577** Francis Drake undertakes the second circumnavigation of the world.

**1580** The crowns of Spain and Portugal unite under Philip II of Spain (formerly the husband of Mary I of England), marking the start of the decline of the Portuguese Empire.

**1581** The Act of Abjuration formally declares the independence of the Dutch Low Countries from Spain.

**1582** A new calendar ('the Gregorian Calendar') is introduced by Pope Gregory XIII, replacing the one which has been in use since the time of Julius Caesar. Not everyone adopts it willingly: Russia and Greece hold out until the early twentieth century.

**1585** Sir Walter Raleigh masterminds an unsuccessful attempt to colonize Virginia in North America.

**1588** The English navy defeats the Spanish Armada, thought by many to be invincible, in the course of a lengthy Anglo-Spanish war.

**1598–1613** Russia's 'Time of Troubles', during which the famine of 1601–3 kills almost 2 million people.

**1600** The British East India Company is established, originally to control all British trade with Asia, but later as a military and political force too.

**1601** English victory in the Battle of Kinsale destroys the power of the traditional Irish chieftains and effectively brings Ireland under English rule.

**1602** The Dutch East India Company is founded and given a monopoly of all Dutch trade in Asia. It rapidly becomes the most important business in the world, making a fortune from the trade in spices.

**1603** The Tokugawa Shogunate takes control of Japan and remains in power until 1868.

**1603** Exit the Tudors, enter the Stuarts. Elizabeth I dies childless. Her cousin, James VI of Scotland, who has held the throne since babyhood and is the son of the beheaded Mary, Queen of Scots, unites the two kingdoms by also becoming James I of England.

**1604** The Treaty of London ends England's hostilities with Spain.

**1606** The Dutch navigator Willem Janszoon gives the first recorded European sighting of mainland Australia.

**1607** Jamestown, Virginia, becomes the first successful English settlement in North America.

**1608** Quebec is founded by the French as a base for exploration and fur trade.

**1609** The first central monetary authority, the Bank of Amsterdam, is founded.

**1613** The House of Romanov is established in Russia, ending the 'Time of Troubles'.

**1618** The Thirty Years' War, fought mainly in Germany but involving almost every major state in Europe, begins.

**1619** The first African slaves arrive in North America.

**1620** The voyage of the *Mayflower*: English pilgrims escaping religious persecution at home land at what becomes Plymouth, Massachusetts, and establish what will be one of the most important European settlements in the New World.

**1622** Native Americans kill a quarter of the English population of Jamestown, Virginia, in the Jamestown Massacre.

**1625** The Dutch West India Company (established in 1621) founds New Amsterdam, later New York.

**1629–42** The 'Great Migration' of some 20,000 Puritans to America from England.

**1634–37** Tulip Mania, one of the world's first recorded economic bubbles, strikes. One speculator offers to exchange five hectares of land for a single bulb. Many misguided souls go bankrupt when the market suddenly collapses.

**1640–68** The Portuguese Restoration War ends the period of dual monarchy with Spain. The Treaty of Lisbon re-establishes Portuguese independence.

**1642** The Dutch explorer Abel Tasman becomes the first recorded European to discover New Zealand and Tasmania.

**1642–48** In England Charles I's persistent ignoring of parliament and his insistence on the king's supreme power leads to civil war.

**1643** Louis XIV accedes to the throne of France. His long reign (lasting until 1715) is a period of absolute rule and military aggression, which causes the rest of Europe to unite against him. It is also a time of absolutism in the Church: in 1685 Louis revokes the almost ninety-year-old Edict of Nantes, which had given Protestants freedom of worship; hundreds of thousands of Huguenots flee the country. Louis' new palace at Versailles is a splendid backdrop for the man who becomes known as 'the Sun King'.

**1644** The Chinese Ming Dynasty is replaced by the Shun Dynasty; it in turn is soon replaced by the Manchu-led Qing Dynasty (which rules until 1911).

**1648** The Peace of Westphalia ends both the Thirty Years' War and the Eighty Years' War between Spain and the Netherlands. Spain now acknowledges Dutch independence, the power of the Holy Roman Empire is weakened and France becomes the dominant power in Europe.

**1649** In England, Charles I is defeated and beheaded. The leader of the Parliamentarians, Oliver Cromwell, becomes Lord Protector of the new Commonwealth.

**1649–53** Cromwell leads the New Model Army to crush a rebellion in Ireland. They haven't forgiven him to this day.

**1652** The Dutch East India Company founds Cape Town.

### The Restoration
After Cromwell's death in 1658 the Commonwealth falls apart and in 1660 Charles I's exiled son is restored to the throne as Charles II. He has innumerable mistresses and likes to enjoy himself: theatres are reopened and bawdy 'Restoration comedies' are performed. On the downside, the Great Plague (1665) and Great Fire of London (1666) occur during Charles's reign. Conflict between Catholics and Protestants continues to simmer.

**1683** The Battle of Vienna marks the end of the Ottoman expansion into Europe.

**1688–89** In Britain, the 'Glorious Revolution' deposes the staunchly Catholic James II; his Protestant daughter and her husband, the Dutch Prince William of Orange, are invited to rule jointly as William and Mary. From this point on, British monarchs are forbidden to be or to marry Catholics.

**1688–1746** The Jacobite Risings attempt to restore James II and his descendants to the thrones of Scotland and England.

**1689** A border is established between China and Russia with the Treaty of Nerchinsk.

### The War of the Spanish Succession

Charles II of Spain dies childless (history would be a lot more peaceful if monarchs learnt not to do that) in 1700. For complicated reasons involving near-incestuous inter-marrying, the royal families of France and Austria – the Bourbons and Habsburgs respectively – both lay claim to the Spanish Empire. War breaks out in 1701 and the British monarchs William III and subsequently Queen Anne play a major negotiating role: the Duke of Marlborough's victory at the Battle of Blenheim is part of this war. It ends in 1713; the upshot is that a grandson of Louis XIV becomes King Philip V of Spain, while most of Spain's other European possessions pass to Austria. Britain makes the strategic move of gaining control of Gibraltar.

**1689** In England, the Bill of Rights lays out certain basic rights of all Englishmen living under a constitutional monarchy.

**1700–21** The Great Northern War ends with Russia (under Peter the Great) outstripping the Swedish Empire as the dominant Baltic power. For the first time, Russia is a major player in European politics.

**1706–07** The Acts of Union unite the Scottish and English parliaments and create the United Kingdom of Great Britain.

**1707** The death of the Mughal leader Aurangzeb sends the Mughal Empire into decline.

**1712** New France (French territory in North America) reaches its peak, stretching from Newfoundland to the Rocky Mountains, and from Hudson Bay to the Gulf of Mexico.

**1720** The South Sea Bubble occurs after the British South Sea Company is granted a monopoly on trade with South America. A boom in the company's stock is followed by financial collapse and an investigation that reveals (how very modern of it) corruption at high levels. Thousands are ruined (a few get very rich).

**1721** Robert Walpole becomes so influential in the British government that he is generally regarded as the first Prime Minister (then called 'First Minister' as the King was still sitting in parliament. The title of Prime Minister doesn't become official until Henry Campbell-Bannerman takes office in 1905).

**1736–96** The Chinese Empire expands to include Tibet, Mongolia, Burma and Nepal.

**1739–48** The War of Jenkins' Ear is fought in the Caribbean between Spain and Britain (and merges into the War of the Austrian Succession); it ends with improved relations between both powers. The name comes from one Captain Robert Jenkins, whose ear was apparently cut off by a Spanish coastguard whom he had insulted.

**1740** Frederick the Great becomes King of Prussia, a German state which at its peak covers much of north-eastern Europe, from Denmark to the Russian border. A cultured 'Renaissance man', patron of writers and musicians, he is also a great soldier who establishes Prussia as a force to be reckoned with.

**1756–63** The Seven Years' War diminishes France's imperial influence, with much of New France divided between Britain and Spain. Britain is established as the world's greatest naval power. The war also increases Prussia's status within central Europe.

**1757** The Battle of Plassey ends in victory for the British East India Company, which gains control of Bengal and from there extends its influence over much of southern Asia, including all of India and what is now Pakistan.

**1770** Captain James Cook lands in Botany Bay, Australia, and claims the east coast for Britain.

**1776** The War of American Independence: British colonies in America revolt against the 'taxation without representation' (i.e. with no representation at Westminster) to which they

## The Enlightenment

The late seventeenth- and eighteenth-century writers and philosophers who formed part of the Enlightenment or Age of Reason – an almost endless list that includes Voltaire and Goethe, to name but two – believed in the supremacy of reason over superstition and emotion, and shared a passionate desire to combat inequality and injustice.

A significant work of the period is Thomas Paine's *The Rights of Man*, written in 1791–2 as a defence of the ideals of the French Revolution. Paine advocated a 'social contract' between government and governed, to be reaffirmed by each generation so that power could not be passed on as of right – a state of affairs that Paine believed would lead to tyranny.

Despite Paine's defence, the excesses of the French Revolution (see **The French Revolution** on page 96) are one of the reasons that the Age of Reason came to an end. The literary and artistic movement known as Romanticism – Wordsworth, Keats, Shelley, etc. – in which emotion came back into fashion, was also a reaction against rationalist ideas. Nevertheless, the Enlightenment is up there with printing and the Reformation in terms of its influence on what came afterwards. In Western Europe at least, the Church was never so powerful again, and emancipation from Church dogma paved the way for many advances in science. The idea that tradition was less important than progress took hold and has remained with us ever since.

have been submitted for many years and on 4 July declare themselves independent. Following the Treaty of Paris (1783) Britain formally relinquishes all claims to the United States.

**1780–84** There has been conflict between the British and the Dutch over trading routes for over a century; now the Fourth Anglo-Dutch War ends disastrously for the Dutch and contributes to the weakening of their power.

**1788** Sydney Bay, Australia, is declared the first British penal colony. From now until 1868, criminals convicted of anything from stealing fish to attempting to start a trade union may be 'transported' to Australia for life.

## The French Revolution

Despotic rule in France has finally gone too far. On 14 July 1789 (still a national holiday in France), the people of Paris storm the prison of the Bastille, a symbol of aristocratic oppression. A constitutional monarchy and later a republican government are established and in 1793 Louis XVI and his queen, Marie Antoinette, are executed. Thousands of suspected anti-revolutionaries also go to the guillotine under the 'Reign of Terror' led by Maximilien Robespierre. The Terror ends with Robespierre's own execution and the establishment of the Directoire, a more moderate but corrupt and incompetent government. In 1799 this is overthrown by an artillery officer named Napoleon Bonaparte, of whom we shall be hearing more ...

**1788** The African Association is formed in Britain to encourage explorers to improve European knowledge of the 'Dark Continent'.

**1789** George Washington becomes the first President of the United States of America.

**1798** The United Irishmen, with some assistance from Revolutionary France, stage an unsuccessful uprising aimed at securing Irish independence from Britain.

**1800** The Dutch East India Company is dissolved.

**1801** An Act of Union proclaims the United Kingdom of Great Britain and Ireland.

**1801–15** The Barbary Wars erupt between the USA and the Barbary States of North Africa over the question of whether or not American trading ships in the Mediterranean should pay tribute to the region's notorious pirates.

**1803** The Louisiana Purchase sees Napoleon sell France's US holdings (an area of over 2 million square kilometres) to the USA for $15 million, more than doubling the area of the United States. This extraordinary deal marks the beginning of the period of American expansion and the end of France's colonial efforts in North America.

**1806** The Holy Roman Empire is dissolved; Napoleon reorganizes parts of it into the Confederation of the Rhine, a group of German states effectively under French rule.

**Napoleon**

In 1804 Napoleon is crowned Emperor of France. It's his own idea. He has conquered much of Europe; before he has finished he will have established his brothers as kings of Spain, Holland and Westphalia and a friend as Crown Prince of Sweden, so of course he needs a grander title than them. He remains at war with Britain and in 1805 is defeated at sea by Admiral Horatio Nelson at the Battle of Trafalgar, where Nelson himself is killed. The Duke of Wellington's army eventually forces Napoleon out of Spain. Napoleon, after brutal failure in Russia in 1812, abdicates in 1814, escapes from his prison on the island of Elba, reclaims power for what is known as the 'Hundred Days' but is finally defeated by Wellington at the Battle of Waterloo in 1815, bringing an end to the Napoleonic Wars. The French monarchy is restored and Napoleon spends the last six years of his life in exile in St Helena, a remote island in the south Atlantic.

**1807** Britain abolishes its slave trade.

**1810–26** The Latin American Wars of Independence lead to freedom (for most colonies) from Spanish and Portuguese control.

## The Industrial Revolution

This series of developments began in Britain in the mid-eighteenth century and spread across the world, changing the economy from an agriculture-based one to a town-based one centred on large-scale manufacturing.

The Industrial Revolution was preceded and made possible by the Agricultural Revolution, which began in the seventeenth century and which had two far-reaching results: one, more food could be produced, so people didn't have to work on the land to feed themselves; and two, people who had lost their jobs on the land moved to town to look for work. The subsequent developments – including mass production, the invention of spinning and weaving machines, and the vast quantity of cheap cotton that was arriving in England from the USA – culminated in the factories of Lancashire standing at the centre of the newly industrialized world.

When the American Civil War broke out in 1861 (see page 104), the supply of cotton became unreliable. Fortunately Britain controlled almost every aspect of trade in India, so that it could import raw cotton and put protective tariffs on Indian calicos, making them too expensive to compete with Manchester-made cloth. Fortunate, too, that the Suez Canal opened in 1869, halving the journey time from India to Britain. A series of happy events that contributed – until the First World War and beyond – to the attitude, held by Britain at least, that Britannia indeed ruled the waves.

**1812–15** War between the British Empire and the United States ends in stalemate and opens a period of peaceful relations between the two.

**1814** Following the (first) fall of Napoleon, the Congress of Vienna redraws European boundaries and in 1815 the German Confederation establishes a union of German-speaking states in order to protect themselves against any further incursions from France.

**1819** Sir Thomas Stamford Raffles founds a British colony at Singapore to help secure a trade route from China to Britain.

**1820** Several explorers claim to have been the first to discover Antarctica.

**1829** Western Australia is claimed by the British.

**1830** In France, the July Revolution deposes Charles X and replaces him with Louis-Philippe, who becomes king not by hereditary right but by popular consent. Perhaps inevitably, popular consent changes its mind and deposes him in 1848. Meanwhile, mirror revolts occur in Belgium (where the present royal family is installed) and in other parts of Europe.

**1833** The Slavery Abolition Act outlaws slavery throughout the British Empire.

**1837** Queen Victoria comes to the throne. Her reign lasts until 1901, and marks a period of great power and prosperity for the British Empire, as well as scientific, industrial and artistic developments at home.

**1840** The Treaty of Waitangi brings New Zealand into the British Empire.

### The First Opium War

Over the years the British East India Company has gone from strength to strength. One of the commodities British traders deal in is opium, which they import illegally from India to China. In 1839 Chinese authorities confiscate 20,000 chests of opium, leading Britain to send warships and threaten various Chinese cities. In 1842 the Treaty of Nanking, which brings this war to an end, cedes the Chinese territory of Hong Kong to Britain, under whose control it remains until 1997. Further opening up of trade with the West is forced on China after the Second Opium War (1856–60).

**1845** The Great Famine strikes Ireland and leads to the death of approximately 1 million people and the emigration of a further 1 million (from a population of *c.* 3 million) over the next five years.

**1845** The phrase 'Manifest Destiny' is coined and popularizes support for US westward expansionism.

**1848** Revolutions erupt across Europe and elsewhere in reaction to dissatisfaction with political leadership and conditions of life.

**1848** Texas, California and New Mexico are incorporated into the United States following the war with Mexico.

**1849** The California Gold Rush brings some 300,000 gold-seekers to the United States.

**1854–56** The Crimean War, fought in the province of Crimea in Ukraine, sees the British, French and Turkish attempt to prevent Russia expanding its control of areas around the Black Sea.

### The Indian Mutiny

Also called the Indian Rebellion or the 1857 War of Independence: Indian soldiers in the Bengal army of the East India Company revolt against their British officers, and the rebellion spreads to the civil population. It is crushed, but the East India Company's power is also destroyed. The British Crown takes over control of India, initiating the period of the Raj (from the Hindu for 'rule'); this continues until 1947, when India becomes independent and two parts of it are 'partitioned' off to create the new state of Pakistan and what is now Bangladesh (formerly East Pakistan).

**1858–61** Russia emancipates its serfs.

### The Unification of Italy

For centuries, Italy has been divided into different kingdoms, duchies and city-states, not to mention the area ruled by the Pope. It has at various times been governed by Spain, Austria and France and, like much of the rest of Europe, invaded by Napoleon. From the 1830s a movement called the Risorgimento ('resurrection') aims to oust foreign rulers and establish a unified state. Prominent figures are the politician Camillo Cavour, the military leader Giuseppe Garibaldi and the king of Piedmont–Sardinia, who becomes Victor Emmanuel II, first King of Italy in 1861. (He's called the second because there had been a Victor Emmanuel I of Sardinia a few generations earlier.)

**1864** The First International – otherwise known as the International Workingmen's Association – is founded in London; its first conference, in Geneva in 1866, gathers together socialists from across Europe.

## The American Civil War

A key issue here is slavery: the northern states are trying to abolish it; the South needs slave labour for its cotton plantations. In 1861 eleven southern states break away from the Union and form a Confederacy. Everything you have seen in *Gone with the Wind* happens during and in the aftermath of this war, including the burning of Atlanta and the battles of Fort Sumter and Gettysburg, where President Abraham Lincoln gives his famous address in 1863. Perhaps half a million Americans are killed before the Confederates surrender in 1865; within a week Lincoln is shot dead by a Confederate sympathizer, John Wilkes Booth.

**1865** The Thirteenth Amendment to the United States Constitution outlaws slavery.

**1868** The Meiji ('enlightened government') Restoration in Japan ends the Tokugawa Shogunate period.

**1870** The Fifteenth Amendment in the United States makes voting a constitutional right regardless of colour.

**1870** The First Vatican Council meets to discuss Church doctrine and practice; its most important outcome is the declaration of papal infallibility.

## The Unification of Germany

Prussia has long been famous for its highly organized army; once Otto von Bismarck becomes minister-president in 1862, it reaches new heights. Bismarck, proclaiming values of 'blood and iron', provokes wars against some of his neighbours, notably France (the Franco-Prussian War, 1870–71), during which he forces the emperor, Napoleon III, into exile, besieges the capital and proclaims victory. The French establish both a moderate provisional government and a short-lived revolutionary version called the Commune, which divides the country and results in bitter fighting in Paris before the *communards* are forced to surrender. In the meantime, Bismarck has proclaimed the Prussian king, William I, German Emperor ('kaiser'). In 1871 Germany as we know it comes into being for the first time.

**1879** The Anglo-Zulu War ends in British victory, though not before an entire British column has been massacred by Zulus, with the loss of some 1,300 lives.

**1880–81** The First Boer War grants the Boers – Dutch-speaking settlers in South Africa – independence from Britain in the region of the Transvaal.

**1882** Germany forms the Triple Alliance with Italy and Austria (later joined by the Ottoman Empire and Bulgaria).

**1880s** The Scramble for Africa: European powers are busily exploiting the continent's resources in terms of minerals, timber and cheap/slave labour. A conference in Berlin in 1884–5 formalizes many claims for territory; over the next twenty years almost all of Africa falls under European dominion. Strangely, the African peoples are not consulted.

### The Meiji Constitution

In 1889 a new constitution in Japan affirms the return to an imperial state after the overthrow of the shoguns, the military class who have ruled Japan for seven centuries. The feudal system is dismantled and a Western-style constitution introduced, but ultimate power still rests with the emperor. Japan now opens up for trade with the rest of the world, which leads it into conflict with China (the Sino-Japanese War, 1894–95) and Russia (Russo-Japanese War, 1904–05). It is victorious on both occasions and gains control of parts of the Asian mainland that will stand it in good stead when the Second World War comes along (see page 114).

**1893** New Zealand becomes the first country to grant women the vote.

**1897** The First Zionist Congress at Basle aims to establish a home for Jews in Palestine.

## The Spanish-American War

If you've ever wondered how the US came to be in charge of Cuba and Puerto Rico, here is your answer. Both islands are Spanish colonies rebelling against the Spanish in the quest for independence; the US supports them, war breaks out in 1898, the Spanish are defeated and the US takes control. It also buys the Philippines from Spain for $12 million – a bargain at about $1,688 per island.

**1898** In Germany Kaiser William II begins an ambitious naval-building programme and the arms race begins.

**1899–1902** British victory in the Second Boer War incorporates the Boer republics, the Transvaal and the Orange Free State into the British Empire.

**1900** The Boxer Uprising in China breaks out in opposition to foreign imperialism.

**1901** Australia is declared a British Dominion. A new city, Canberra, is built as the capital because no one is brave enough to choose between Sydney and Melbourne.

**1904** A series of agreements known as the Entente Cordiale is signed by Britain and France. Russian joins in 1907 to form the Triple Entente.

**1907** New Zealand becomes a self-governing dominion.

**1910** The Union of South Africa is formed from the four previously independent provinces.

**1911–12** The Chinese Revolution brings an end to imperial rule and creates a republic.

**1912–13** The Balkan Wars almost eradicate the Ottoman Empire from Europe.

### The First World War

Conflicts of interest between Germany, Austro-Hungary and Turkey (the Central Powers) on the one hand and Britain, France and Russia (the Allied Powers) on the other mean that war has been on the cards for some time. It is finally sparked by the assassination of the heir to the Austro-Hungarian throne, the Archduke Franz Ferdinand in 1914. Much of the war is fought on the Western Front (north-eastern France and Belgium) where the 1916 Battle of the Somme, with over a million casualties, remains one of the bloodiest of all time. After the Allied victory in 1918, by which point the USA had joined the war on the Allied side, the peace treaty signed at Versailles in 1919, including the first ever 'war guilt' clause, humiliates Germany and is instrumental in the rise of Hitler, who promises to restore national pride. The end of the war also sees the collapse of the Austro-Hungarian and Ottoman (Turkish) empires (see **The Modern Arab World** on page 110).

**1914** The Panama Canal opens, allowing easy passage between the Atlantic and Pacific Oceans.

**1914** The Home Rule Act grants a limited form of self-government to Ireland, although it's deferred until after the war.

**1916** The Easter Rising in Dublin sees a failed attempt by radical republican groups to proclaim an Irish Republic.

**1917** The Russian Revolution: not the first (there was one in 1905) but the most decisive, the root cause being the extreme poverty of the vast majority of the people. In fact there are two 1917 revolutions: in February a mass uprising forces the Tsar to abdicate; in October the Bolsheviks under Lenin (Vladimir Ilyich Ulyanov) attempt to establish a communist state. Vicious civil war follows, ending in 1921 with a communist victory and the creation of the Union of Soviet Socialist Republics (USSR).

**1918–20** The Spanish flu pandemic kills 50–100 million people. Even the lower estimate makes this vastly more than were killed in the First World War (an estimated 16.5 million).

**The Modern Arab World**

During the First World War the Allied Powers begin an informal occupation of the Ottoman Empire; their efforts see its vast collection of territories transformed into a raft of new nations, laying the foundations for the modern Arab world. The 1916 Sykes Picot agreement brings present-day Iraq, Jordan, Israel and the West Bank (Ottoman Mesopotamia) under British control; the same agreement grants the French control of present-day Syria, Lebanon and parts of south-eastern Turkey (Ottoman Syria). Although Turkey manages to break away (see **1923**, opposite), other countries within the dissolved empire take longer to wrestle free. In 1917 the Balfour Declaration has publicly indicated Britain's support for the creation of a Jewish homeland in Palestine (now Israel). Significantly, under British rule, which begins formally in 1922, Palestine witnesses a substantial influx of Jewish immigrants, intent on establishing their own state amid an atmosphere of heightened anti-Semitism across Europe. British rule ends in 1948 and the state of Israel is declared, by which point relations between non-Jewish Palestinians and Jewish settlers has irretrievably broken down. The foundations for the Arab-Israeli conflict as we know it have been laid.

**1920** The League of Nations meets for the first time. Established under the terms of the Treaty of Versailles, it is the first ever international organization dedicated to preserving world peace. Never a great success, it is officially dissolved after the Second World War and replaced by the United Nations.

**1921** The Anglo-Irish Treaty grants separate dominion status to Ireland with the exception of six counties in Ulster: these become 'Northern Ireland' and remain part of the United Kingdom.

**1922** Benito Mussolini, head of the National Fascist Party, becomes Prime Minister of Italy.

**1923** After a three-year war of independence (against the Allies, which had taken control after the First World War), Turkey is declared a republic.

**1926** The Imperial Conference establishes the principle that all the British dominions are made equal in status to the UK, rather than sudordinate to it, as had previously been the case.

**1928** The Representation of the People Act in Britain finally allows women in England to vote on equal terms as men.

**1928** In the USSR, Joseph Stalin introduces the first of his series of Five-Year Plans of modernization.

**The Wall Street Crash**

In 1929 the New York stock market collapses, losing 40 per cent of its value in a month and sparking what becomes known as the Great Depression. Unemployment in the US reaches 14 million (the total population is 122 million), banks close and property values plummet. Knock-on effects are felt across the world. American banks no longer lend money to Germany to help with their 'war reparation' payments; the German economy implodes, inflation goes through the roof and 6 million people are unemployed. Politically extreme nationalist movements have emerged in many countries – notably Germany and Italy.

**1931** Mao Zedong proclaims the Jiangxi Soviet, a communist republic within China from which he leads a rebellion against the ruling nationalist party, the Kuomintang. In 1934 the Kuomintang forces the communists out of Jiangxi and 100,000 people, under Mao's leadership, set off on 'the Long March' to Yan'an, 10,000 km away, which then becomes their capital. Mao's status as communist leader is confirmed. The Second World War interrupts the Chinese Civil War, which is resumed in 1945: in 1949 Mao becomes leader of the People's Republic of China and the Kuomintang withdraws to Taiwan.

**Adolf Hitler**

In 1933 Hitler, having risen rapidly through the ranks of the National Socialist (Nazi) Party, becomes Chancellor of Germany and is soon head of a one-party state, eliminating his rivals in the 'Night of the Long Knives' of 1934. German rearmament contravenes the Treaty of Versailles (see **The First World War** on page 108), but Hitler nevertheless rebuilds the armed forces and starts annexing various parts of central Europe, notably Austria and the Sudetenland (a part of Czechoslovakia in which many ethnic Germans live). He also sets about 'purifying' the German race, most notoriously by persecuting Jews: *Kristallnacht* (also referred to as the 'Night of Broken Glass') in November 1938 is a series of attacks against Jewish businesses, homes and synagogues as a result of which tens of thousands of Jews are transported to concentration camps.

**1935** Italy invades the independent African kingdom of Abyssinia (now Ethiopia), in breach of League of Nations rules.

**1936–39** The Spanish Civil War, a bitter conflict between right and left, draws international participation from Russia, Germany and Italy. The Fascist Francisco Franco emerges victorious.

**1937** The second Sino-Japanese War, the result of Japanese encroachment on Chinese territory, and featuring much brutality by the Japanese army, ends only with the surrender of Japan in 1945 (see **The Second World War**, below).

**1938** The Munich Conference: Britain and France, fearing another war, attempt to 'appease' Hitler by granting him rights in the territories he has annexed (see **Adolf Hitler** on page 113). British Prime Minister Neville Chamberlain

**The Second World War**

Britain and France, having guaranteed Polish neutrality, are obliged to declare war on Germany in 1939. Hitler invades France, which falls in 1940, as do Holland, Belgium, Denmark and Norway; he then threatens to invade Britain and subjects it to the bombing attacks known as the Blitz. The war in the air that follows is known as the Battle of Britain. Hitler invades Russia; Russia joins the war on the Allied side. The Japanese, seeking to protect their own interests in eastern Asia, bomb the US naval base at Pearl Harbor in Hawaii without warning. This brings the US into the conflict, creating a truly world war. In Europe the Normandy landings of June 1944 ('D-Day') turn the tide against Germany, which surrenders in May 1945 ('VE Day'). In August, the Americans drop the first atom bombs, on Hiroshima and Nagasaki; Japan surrenders shortly afterwards.

returns from Munich claiming that there will be 'peace for our time'. Nevertheless, within a year, Hitler has invaded Poland, precipitating the outbreak of the Second World War (see opposite).

# FRENCH

The British are notoriously poor with languages, though this is presumably a hangover from an arrogant imperialistic age rather than a genuine genetic failing. Since the collapse of the Empire, we have had the fact that English is the international language of science, aviation and commerce; the spread of American films and television; and now the internet as our excuse for assuming that 'everyone speaks English'. But just in case you are one of the few who are ashamed of this attitude, or you did a bit of French at school and would like to brush up, or you want to cope a little better on holiday, here – in accordance with the 'just trying to be helpful' attitude on which this book is based – are a few basics.

## MASCULINE AND FEMININE

One of the first things to get to grips with in French is that there is more than one word for 'the' and 'a'. Like lots of other things in this sex-crazed language, these words change according to the gender (masculine or feminine) and the number (singular or plural) of the noun that follows.

For *the*:

> *le* is masculine singular
> *la* is feminine singular

*l'* is used in front of a vowel or silent *h* for both genders

*les* is plural for both genders

For *a*:

*un* is masculine singular

*une* is feminine singular

*des* is plural for both genders

But what is this gender business? Well, all nouns in French are either masculine or feminine. And, in answer to your next question, they just are, OK? Some of this is logical: it's no surprise to find that the word for a man (*un homme*) is masculine or for a woman (*une femme*) is feminine; it's worth remembering that many abstract nouns are feminine (*la beauté, la folie, la politesse* – beauty, madness, politeness), but very often there is no logic to it. An armchair (*un fauteuil*) is masculine; an upright chair (*une chaise*) feminine. A house (*une maison*) is feminine, a flat (*un appartement*) masculine. You just have to accept the concept and learn the article with the noun as you improve your vocabulary.

## Adjectives agree too

Like the articles, adjectives agree with the nouns they describe. In the simplest instances, adding an *e* at the end makes an adjective feminine, and adding an *s* makes it plural, but there are plenty of exceptions:

The word for good, *bon*, becomes *bonne* in the feminine. Similarly *breton, bretonne* (Breton, from Brittany), *mignon, mignonne* (cute) and others.

An adjective ending in *–eux* takes the same form in the singular and the plural; to make it feminine change the ending to *–euse* and to make that plural add an *s*. For example, the word for happy is *heureux* (silent *h*, silent *x*, so pronounced along the lines of *err-err*), but it is modified like this:

> *Un homme heureux* (a happy man)
> *Des hommes heureux* (some happy men)
> *Une femme heureuse* (a happy woman – this time you do pronounce the ending, to get something like *err-errs*)
> *Des femmes heureuses* (some happy women)

The same applies to *généreux* (generous), *prétentieux* (pretentious), *silencieux* (silent) and many more.

> *Doux* (sweet) becomes *douce* in the feminine singular, *doux* and *douces* in the plural.

Possessive adjectives also agree with the noun to which they refer, which can be confusing for English speakers. In English, the 'his' in *he spoke to his wife* is masculine because it refers back to the subject, *he*. In French, this becomes *il a parlé à sa femme*, with the *sa* (feminine) referring to *femme*. Thus *son* (masculine), *sa* (feminine) and *ses* (plural for both genders) can mean either his or hers, depending on the context:

> *Il a besoin de laver sa chemise* (He needs to wash *his* shirt, but *chemise* is feminine)
> *Elle a perdu son manteau* (She has lost *her* overcoat, but *manteau* is masculine)

*Il veut parler à ses filles* (He wants to talk to *his* daughters)
*Elle est allée au cinéma avec ses frères* (she went to the cinema with *her* brothers)

## A bit more about adjectives and adverbs

In French all but the shortest adjectives – and all adjectives of colour (see **L'arc-en-ciel** on page 120), however short they are – follow the noun. You can have *une bonne idée* (a good idea), but if you want to be more enthusiastic it becomes *une idée superbe, une idée géniale* (brilliant) or *une idée sensationelle*.

The vast majority of French adverbs end in *–ment* (the equivalent of the English *–ly*) tacked on to the feminine form of an adjective: *seul, seule, seulement* (only), *lent, lente, lentement* (slow[ly]), *joyeux, joyeuse, joyeusement* (joyful[ly]). When the adjective ends in *–ant* or *–ent* (*élégant, récent*, both meaning what they look as if they mean), this is transformed into an extra *m* to produce the adverbs *élégamment* and *récemment*.

## QUICK PRONUNCIATION GUIDE

There are many ways in which French differs from English, but here are a few of the most basic:

● Don't pronounce the *s* at the end of a word: *je suis* (I am) is *swee*. The verbal part of *tu appelles* (you call) is pronounced the same way as *il appelle* (he calls).

**L'arc-en-ciel**

It means 'the rainbow' (literally 'the arch in the sky'), so here is a list of its colours:

>*rouge* – red
>
>*orange* – orange
>
>*jaune* – yellow
>
>*vert* – green
>
>*bleu* – blue
>
>*bleu indigo* (as you've seen in the Science section, see page 74, indigo is a made-up colour – that's obviously what the French think, anyway)
>
>*violet* – violet

You might also find it useful to memorize:

>*blanc* – white
>
>*noir* – black
>
>*brun* – brown
>
>*gris* – grey

For the ones that don't already end in *e*, add an *e* to make them feminine, except for *violet*, which becomes *violette*, and *blanc*, which becomes *blanche*. And if you want to describe the shade just tag on *clair* (light) or *foncé* (dark) after the colour.

- Don't pronounce the *e* at the end of a word unless it has an accent on it: *appelle* is pronounce *a-pell*; the past participle 'called' is *appelé* (*app-lay*).

- Don't pronounce the *–ent* at the end of a third person plural (*ils appellent*): this too comes out as *a-pell*.

- The *–ez* at the end of a second person singular (*vous appelez*) is pronounced like the *ay* in *play*.

- The final consonant of a word is often silent. *Fond* (bottom, base) is approximately *fon*; *placard* (cupboard) is *plack-arr*. The last syllable of verbs ending in *–er*, such as *donner* (to give) and *arriver* (to arrive), is pronounced *ay* as in *play*. *Forêt* (forest) is quite like the English *foray*.

- Do pronounce the consonant at the end of verbs such as *venir* (to come) – this is *–eer*.

- With words ending in a single *n* such as *bon* (good), *raison* (reason), *faisan* (pheasant), the *n* is swallowed up into a nasal vowel sound often satirized as 'tray bong' for *très bon* (very good) or 'voo savvy raisong' for *vous avez raison* (you're right).

- Before an *a, o* or *u*, a *g* is hard, as in the English *get*. Before an *e* or an *i* it is a softer sound, often shown in dictionaries as *zh*, like the *s* in *treasure*. (The letter *j* is also always pronounced this way.) To harden a *g* before an *e* or an *i*, add a *u*, as in *guerre* (war), which is pronounced *gare* (to rhyme with English *hare*), not *gware*. To keep the *zh* sound in front of an *a*, *o* or *u*, add an *e*. The first person plural of the verb *manger* (to eat, pronounced *mon-zhay*) is *mangeons*, pronounced *mon-zhon*, not *mon-zhay-on*).

Similarly, a *c* in front of an *a*, *o* or *u* is a hard sound, as in *cat*; in front of an *e* or *i* it is soft, as in *centre*. To soften a hard *c*, use a cedilla (*ç*), as in *garçon* (boy or waiter). To harden a soft one, change it to *qu*: the second person plural of *vaincre* (to conquer) is *vous vainquez*, pronounced *van-kay*. *Qu*, which is often the beginning of questioning words *(qui* = who, *quoi* = what) is pronounced as a *k*.

## VERBS

French verbs are conjugated (which means that their endings change according to tense, number and person) in a more complicated way than English ones.

There are two regular forms, with infinitives ending *–er* and *–ir*. To take an example from each, the present tenses look like this:

### *donner* – to give

| | |
|---|---|
| *je donne* | *nous donnons* |
| *tu donnes* | *vous donnez* |
| *il/elle donne* | *ils/elles donnent* |

## Personal pronouns

To make sense of the lists of verbs, it will help you to know the French subject pronouns:

> *je* (abbreviated to *j'* before a vowel) = I
> *tu* = you (informal singular)
> *il* = he
> *elle* = she
> *nous* = we
> *vous* = you (plural or formal singular)
> *ils* = they (masculine)
> *elles* = they (feminine)

*Il* and *elle* may also mean 'it' when they refer to a non-personal noun. Because all nouns are either masculine or feminine, there is no exact equivalent of the neuter 'it'.

The concept of a formal and informal form of 'you' was dropped from English when we stopped using *thou*, but it's important in French. Use *tu* for friends and family, children, animals, anyone you know well. Otherwise – in shops, restaurants, the bank, with your friends' parents and in business correspondence – use *vous*. You may then be invited to be less formal, but if in doubt it's better to err on the side of courtesy.

### *finir* – **to finish**

| | |
|---|---|
| *je finis* | *nous finissons* |
| *tu finis* | *vous finissez* |
| *il/elle finit* | *ils/elles finissent* |

Verbs whose infinitives end in *–re* tend to mess about with their middle consonants, but follow a sort of pattern:

### *craindre* – **to fear**

| | |
|---|---|
| *je crains* | *nous craignons* |
| *tu crains* | *vous craignez* |
| *il/elle craint* | *ils/elles craignent* |

### *prendre* – **to take**

| | |
|---|---|
| *je prends* | *nous prenons* |
| *tu prends* | *vous prenez* |
| *il/elle prend* | *ils/elles prennent* |

### *vivre* – **to live**

| | |
|---|---|
| *je vis* | *nous vivons* |
| *tu vis* | *vous vivez* |
| *il/elle vit* | *ils/elles vivent* |

You get the hang of them eventually.

## Irregular verbs

In many languages, the most common verbs are the most irregular, and French is no exception. Here are the present tenses of four of the oddest:

### *être* – to be

| | |
|---|---|
| *je suis* | *nous sommes* |
| *tu es* | *vous êtes* |
| *il/elle est* | *ils/elles sont* |

### *avoir* – to have

| | |
|---|---|
| *j'ai* | *nous avons* |
| *tu as* | *vous avez* |
| *il/elle a* | *ils/elles ont* |

### *aller* – to go

| | |
|---|---|
| *je vais* | *nous allons* |
| *tu vas* | *vous allez* |
| *il/elle va* | *ils/elles vont* |

### *faire* – to do, to make

| | |
|---|---|
| *je fais* | *nous faisons* |
| *tu fais* | *vous faisez* |
| *il/elle fait* | *ils/elles font* |

## Past tense

The past tense most commonly used in conversation is the perfect – the equivalent of the English 'I have carried', 'you have followed', etc., but also of 'I carried', 'you followed' if this was a one-off occurrence in the recent past. In French this is normally formed with the verb *avoir* (to have), so that 'I (have) carried' becomes *j'ai porté* and 'you (have) followed' translates as *tu as suivi*. But there is a handful of verbs, most of them expressing movement, but also the verbs for 'to be born' and 'to die', that are conjugated with *être*. In olden days, students of French would have learnt these by rote, so here they are in case you want to do the same:

*aller* – to go

*arriver* – to arrive

*descendre* – to descend, get down from (a vehicle)

*devenir* – to become

*entrer* – to enter

*monter* – to climb, get up into (a vehicle)

*mourir* – to die

*naître* – to be born

*partir* – to leave, depart

*rentrer* – to re-enter

*rester* – to stay

*retourner* – to return

*revenir* – to come back

*sortir* – to go out

*tomber* – to fall

*venir* – to come

The complication here is that when verbs are conjugated with *être*, the past participle agrees with the subject. So although *j'ai mangé* remains the same whether the speaker is masculine or feminine, *je suis parti* becomes *je suis partie* if the speaker is female; in the plural it would be *nous sommes partis* or *nous sommes parties*. Women's lib has not caught up with French grammar: the masculine is said to embrace the feminine, so that a group of ten people of whom nine were female would still require a masculine adjective or pronoun.

## Negatives

English expresses a negative with the word *not* (often abbreviated to *n't* in *won't, can't, don't*, etc). In French you need two words for the same thing – *ne* before the verb (abbreviated to *n'* if the verb begins with a vowel) and *pas* after it.

| | |
|---|---|
| *Je parle français* | *Je ne parle pas français* |
| (I speak French) | (I don't speak French) |
| *Il est là* | *Il n'est pas là* |
| (he is there) | (he isn't there) |

Other negative expressions also require *ne*, so that French insists on a double negative that would be incorrect in English:

*Tu ne réponds jamais* (you never answer)
*Il n'a rien dit* (he didn't say anything)
*Nous n'avons aucune idée* (we have no idea)

### Répondez s'il vous plaît

We've all seen RSVP on invitations, but how many of us realize why it means what it means? *S'il vous plaît* is the common French expression for 'please', but it means literally 'if it pleases you' and introduces another useful grammatical point. Where we would say, 'I like such-and-such', the French often say, 'Such-and-such pleases me' and the verb is singular or plural depending on what the such-and-such is.

*La musique de Mozart me plaît* (I like Mozart's music, singular)

but

*Les opéras de Mozart me plaisent* (I like Mozart's operas, plural)

# DAY-TO-DAY VOCABULARY

Excuse the lists, but sometimes you do just have to cut to the chase and learn stuff by heart.

**Days of the week** (starting with Sunday): *dimanche, lundi, mardi, mercredi, jeudi, vendredi, samedi.*

**Months of the year:** *janvier, février, mars, avril, mai, juin, juillet, août, septembre, octobre, novembre, décembre.*

Note that these don't begin with a capital letter in French. Nor do languages or nationalities: *l'anglais* is English (the language), *un mot anglais* is an English word, *une voiture anglaise* an English car. But when the adjective becomes a noun, then it does need a capital: 'there were three people in the room, two Frenchmen and a German' would be *Il y avait trois personnes dans la salle, deux Français et un Allemand.*

**Numbers up to twenty:** *un, deux, trois, quatre, cinq, six, sept, huit, neuf, dix, onze, douze, treize, quatorze, quinze, seize, dix-sept, dix-huit, dix-neuf, vingt.*

**Dates:** these are expressed as *le premier janvier, le deux septembre, le dix-sept décembre*, etc. *Premier* means first, but for all other dates the cardinal (two, three, four) rather than the ordinal (second, third, fourth) number is used.

**Time and weather:** French has no exact equivalent of *o'clock.* Time is expressed as *une heure, deux heures* (literally 'one hour, two hours', but meaning 'one o'clock, two o'clock'), etc. Half past one is *une heure et demie*; quarter to and quarter past are respectively *une heure moins* (less) *le quart* and *une heure et quart.* To ask someone the time, say *Quelle heure est-il?* (What time is it?) or *Avez-vous l'heure?* (Do you have the time?) Tacking *s'il vous plaît* on the end will do no harm.

The word *temps* also means time, so you could ask, *Avez-vous le temps de venir avec moi?* (Do you have time to come with me?) But *Quel temps fait-il?* means 'What's the weather like?' Answers might include:

| | |
|---|---|
| *Il fait beau* | It's fine |
| *Il fait du soleil* | It's sunny |
| *Il pleut* | It's raining |
| *Il neige* | It's snowing |
| *Il fait du vent* | It's windy |
| *Il fait chaud* | It's hot |
| *Il fait froid* | It's cold |

Note the use of the verb *faire* (to make) where we would use *to be.*

Other instances in which French uses a different verb from English are:

*J'ai chaud* – I'm hot (literally I have heat)
*J'ai froid* – I'm cold (I have cold)
*J'ai faim* – I'm hungry (I have hunger)
*J'ai soif* – I'm thirsty (I have thirst)
*J'ai peur* – I'm frightened (I have fear)
*J'ai raison* – I'm right (I have right/reason)
*J'ai tort* – I'm wrong (I have wrong)

## Members of the family

*un père* – father
*une mère* – mother
*un fils* – son
*une fille* – daughter
*un frère* – brother
*une soeur* – sister
*les parents* – the parents
*les enfants* – the children
*le grand-père* – grandfather
*la grand-mère* – grandmother

but, more logically than in English, given that *petit* means 'little':

> *le petit-fils, la petite-fille, les petits-enfants* – grandson, granddaughter, grandchildren.

The hyphen is important, because without it these expressions would mean 'the little boy, the little girl, the little children'.

Oddly and potentially confusingly, both 'in-law' and 'step' are conveyed by the adjective for handsome or beautiful, *beau* or *belle*. So *un beau-père, une belle-mère, un beau-fils, une belle-fille, un beau-frère* and *une belle-soeur* could be respectively a father-, mother-, son-, daughter-, brother- and sister-in-law or a 'step' version of any of those relationships.

## A TOURIST'S PHRASE LIST

*La plume de ma tante est sur la table* and *elle a des idées au dessus de sa gare* are clichés from an early era and frankly I have no idea how to say, 'My postilion has been struck by lightning' in French. So here instead are some tips for basic communication while on holiday.

### Greetings

The French address strangers as *monsieur* or *madame* much more than the English would use *sir* or *madam*. So always start with, '*Bonjour, monsieur/madame*. After about 6 p.m. *bonjour* becomes *bonsoir* (good evening). *Bonne nuit* (goodnight) is a farewell in French as it is in English; earlier in the day you may like to wish someone *bonne journée*, which is less of a cliché in French than 'Have a nice day' is in English.

Introducing or being introduced? *Je m'appelle* means 'I am (called), my name is' and *Comment vous appelez-vous?* is 'What's your name?' *Enchanté de faire votre connaissance* ('delighted to meet you') is formal but polite; a simple *Enchanté* is fine. *Puis-je vous présenter ma mère?* (May I introduce my mother?) is correct in a formal context; otherwise say, *Voici mon amie Jeanne* (This is my friend Jane).

The French never say *Allô* except on the phone. It's always *Bonjour*, except in very casual conversation, when you might use *Salut* as both 'Hi' and 'Bye'.

And, while on the subject of the phone, it is worth mentioning two expressions that are often spoken so quickly they leave you gasping for air. The first is *Qui est à l'appareil?*, which means 'Who's speaking?' (Yes, I know you were taught that *un appareil* was a camera, but that is *un appareil de photo* as opposed to *un appareil de téléphone*.)

The second is *Ne quittez pas*, which literally means 'Don't leave' but in this context asks you to hold on. You may also be asked to *patientez un peu*, be patient, bear with me, I'll just have to look at the diary, that sort of thing.

## Booking a hotel

Swot up on the numbers and the days of the week listed on page 128, then ask something like, *Est-ce que vous avez une chambre pour deux personnes pour le 15 et 16 septembre?* With or without a bathroom would be *avec* or *sans salle de bain* (or possible just *bain*). *Douche* means a shower. Breakfast (*petit déjeuner*) may or may not be included: ask *Est-ce que le petit déjeuner est compris?*

Lunch and dinner are respectively *le déjeuner* and *le dîner*.

## In a restaurant

Any guidebook will give you a list of foods and drinks from *huîtres* (oysters) to *gâteau St Honoré* (a truly decadent dessert made with little puffs of choux pastry sandwiched together with *crème patissière* – save room for it). But here are a few more everyday words:

| | |
|---|---|
| *café (au lait)* | (white) coffee |
| *thé* | tea |
| *tisane* | herbal tea |
| *lait (froid/chaud)* | (cold/hot) milk |
| *bière* | beer |

| | |
|---|---|
| *eau (gazeuse)* | (sparkling) water |
| *vin (rouge/blanc)* | (red/white) wine |

Since the people of the Champagne region became so possessive about their name, any other sparkling wine is likely to be described as *crémant* or *pétillant*.

Although *une boisson* is a drink, you are more likely to be offered *quelque-chose à boire* – something to drink. If you've had a round of drinks and want to order the same again, ask for *la même chose*.

| | |
|---|---|
| *pain* | bread |
| *beurre* | butter |
| *fromage* | cheese |
| *viande* | meat |
| *poulet* | chicken |
| *porc* | pork |
| *boeuf* | beef |
| *agneau* | lamb |
| *saignant* | rare |
| *pas trop bien cuit* | medium rare |
| *à point* | medium |
| *bien cuit* | well done |
| *légumes* | vegetables |
| *pommes de terres* | (often abbreviated to *pommes*, though this is also the word for apples) potatoes |
| *pommes frites* | fried potatoes (chips) |
| *petits pois* | peas |
| *haricots (verts)* | (green) beans |
| *chou* | cabbage |

The French are not renowned for helping the English understand their language, but just occasionally they relent and use words such as *carrottes*, *salade* and *fruits*. Fruits include *oranges* and *bananes* as well as *pommes*, but also *framboises* (raspberries), *fraises* (strawberries) and *cassis* (blackcurrants – *crème de cassis* is the liqueur used in Kir.)

The menu is *la carte* (as in *à la carte*); a *menu* (pronounced with the emphasis on the second syllable, something like *m'noo*) is a set menu, with a limited choice and a fixed price.

Do not, whatever you have seen in 1950s films, address a waiter as *garçon*: to attract attention, call out *S'il vous plaît*. And when it's time for the bill, ask for *l'addition* in a restaurant, *la note* in a hotel.

## Travel

A railway station is *une gare*; *une station* is used for stops on the Paris Métro, for a taxi rank or a bus depot; an individual bus stop is *un arrêt*. A ticket is *un billet,* one way is *aller simple* and return is *un billet aller-retour*. French railway stations often confuse novices by not having ticket barriers but insisting instead that you *compostez* your ticket – stick it in a machine on the platform that will punch it and date-stamp it before you board. (Look out for these machines – getting on a train without composting your ticket seems to be every bit as serious as getting on without a ticket at all.)

# WRITTEN COMMUNICATION

If you're feeling confident, why not have a go at some written French ...

## Letters

In the most formal business letters, French doesn't use 'dear' – it cracks straight in with *'Monsieur'*, *'Madame'* or *'Messieurs'* (the equivalent of 'Dear Sirs', which you might use if you were writing to a company). Once you have established a relationship, even a formal, business one, you can write to *'Cher Monsieur'* or *'Chère Madame Dupont'*. You'd use this form, too, if you were writing to someone you knew but were on formal terms with: a friend's parent, the head of your child's school, etc. *Cher Alain, Chère Sophie* is used, as it is in English, for anyone with whom you are on first-name terms. *Mon cher* or *ma chère*, followed by the given name, is a little more intimate, again as it would be in English.

Ways of signing off a formal letter can be as long as the letter itself, but if you master these two you won't go far wrong:

> *Veuillez agréer, Monsieur, l'expression de mes sentiments distingués.*

> *Dans l'attente de vous lire, je vous prie d'agréer, Messieurs, l'expression de mes sentiments distingués.*

Despite appearances, the first boils down to nothing more complicated than 'Yours faithfully' or 'Yours sincerely', and the second to 'I look forward to hearing from you. Yours faithfully/sincerely'.

For friendlier letters, try:

> *Salutations distinguées*
> *Cordialement*
> *Amicalement*
> *Bien à vous*
> *Affectueusement*
> *Je t'embrasse*
> *Grosses bises*
> *Bisous*

These are in ascending order of intimacy from 'warm greetings' to 'love and kisses'. *Bise* and *bisou* are both informal, casual variations of the word *baiser*, to kiss. Be careful how you use that one: although *baiser la main d'une dame* means literally 'to kiss a lady's hand', the verb has drifted into slang use to suggest that the hand-kissing stage was a little while ago.

## E-speak

English has always infiltrated the French language – despite the efforts of the Académie française and other purists, *le weekend*, *le parking* and *le camping* are everywhere. Come the electronic age, of course, the infiltration has become all the more powerful, and English (or American or international-speak) prevails. *Internet* (rather than *l'internet*) is the standard word and 'on line' is *en ligne*, a literal translation. Email is strictly speaking *courrier électronique* ('electronic mail'), abbreviated to *courriel*, but *email* will do nicely. And you can send *un texto* on your (*téléphone*) *portable*.

If you are texting, here are a few useful abbrevs:

> A+ = *à plus tard* (see you later)
> C1blag = *C'est une blague* (just kidding)
> DQP = *dès que possible* (ASAP)
> KOI29 = *Quoi de neuf?* (what's new?)
> MDR = *mort de rire* (dying with laughter)
> MR6 = *merci* (thanks)
> TOK = *tu OK?* (Are you OK?)

On which friendly note it seems only appropriate to say, 'ALP.' That's *à la prochaine*, 'till the next time' and can be translated in text-speak as 'TTFN, ta ta for now'.

# GEOGRAPHY

Geography is probably the most wide-ranging subject in this book; indeed, geographers will tell you it is the most wide-ranging subject in the world, as it includes aspects of geology, meteorology, economics, sociology and much else besides. We can't hope to cover all of it in this little chapter, so let's concentrate on the most obvious aspects of things that are all around us: weather and the way the earth is put together.

## CLIMATE AND WEATHER

Because some people are vague about the difference between climate and weather, here are two definitions, courtesy of *Collins English Dictionary*:

**Climate:** the long-term prevalent weather conditions of an area, determined by latitude, position relative to oceans or continents, altitude, etc.

**Weather:** the day-to-day meteorological conditions, especially temperature, cloudiness and rainfall, affecting a specific place.

In other words, *climate* is what it is generally or typically like; *weather* is what it is doing today. So the first questions are: why do they do what they do? Why should latitude make any difference? Oh and hang on, what was latitude again?

## Latitude

Latitude: an angular distance in degrees north or south of the equator (the band round the middle of the earth that joins points that are equidistant from the North and South Poles).

The equator is at latitude 0°. North of it is the northern hemisphere (*hemi* meaning half), south of it the southern hemisphere. The North and South Poles are 90° north or south of the equator, so from North Pole to South Pole is 180° in latitude. Think of it as a semicircle of the earth: if, having travelled from the North to the South Pole you kept going and went up the earth the other side, you would complete a circle of 360°. Latitude is the measurement that is connected with climate; for longitude and its connection with time, see page 144.

### The main lines of latitude

In addition to the equator, there are four main lines of latitude: the tropics of Cancer (23.5°N) and Capricorn (23.5°S), and the Arctic and Antarctic Circles (66.5° N and S respectively). The area nearest the equator, bounded by the two tropics, is ... well ... the tropics, characterized by high temperatures, often heavy rainfall and two seasons, a wet and a dry. Between the tropics and the polar circles are the temperate zones, with generally mild, unextreme weather and four distinct seasons. North of the Arctic Circle and south of the Antarctic Circle are the polar regions or frigid zones, much of which are permanently frozen.

## The seasons

The earth, as I am sure you know, is a not-quite-perfect sphere, it goes round the sun in an elliptical orbit (an elongated circle) and as it does so it does not stand up straight but tilts at an angle of approximately 23.5°. The orbit takes about a year; this and the tilt combine to produce the seasons. At the same time the earth is rotating on its own axis, taking about twenty-four hours, and this produces night and day.

At different points in the earth's orbit, different parts of its surface are tilting towards or away from the sun. When the northern hemisphere tilts towards the sun, the sun's rays hit it more directly, bringing warmer, sunnier weather and longer days – summer. At the same time, the southern hemisphere is tilting away from the sun, whose rays are hitting it more obliquely – winter.

The higher the latitude you are at the more extreme this effect is, hence the six months of light, six months of dark experienced at the poles. The equator, being in the middle, is not affected by the tilt in the same way. It gets more or less the same amount of **insolation** (incoming solar radiation) year-round and day length remains much the same.

## Wind factors (not necessarily chill)

Another important factor in determining climate is the movement of air. The basic rule from which everything else follows is that warm air rises, because it is less dense and therefore lighter than cool air. As it rises it cools and becomes less able to hold water vapour. Any vapour it is carrying condenses, forms clouds and may subsequently fall as what the weather people call precipitation (rain, snow, hail and the like). Thus the air over the equator is hot (because of insolation) and moist (because it has the capacity to evaporate water and hold it as vapour). As it rises and cools, the vapour condenses and falls as the heavy rain that has produced the lush tropical rainforests. Rainforest plants (like all plants) give off water in a process called transpiration, which contributes to the moisture in the air and thus to the continuing rain which maintains the forests – and so the cycle continues.

## High and low pressure

Where air rises, atmospheric pressure is low. Where it falls, atmospheric pressure is high. And because nature abhors any difference between anything and anything, air from high-pressure areas rushes into low-pressure areas to even things out. It is then warmed, begins to rise and more air comes in to replace it, forming a never-ending cycle called a convection current (see page 76). To complicate matters, the winds in each hemisphere blow not in one big circle but in three big loops or cells. The ones nearest the equator (both north and south) rise about 10–15 km from the earth's surface, where they hit a sort of atmospheric glass ceiling. This forces them to spread out, to latitudes up to 30° north and south, where they cool and sink and, since they have already dropped their vapour as rain, form dry high-pressure areas. This goes some way towards explaining the existence of vast deserts such as the Sahara and the 'Empty Quarter' of Arabia about 30° north of the equator and the Australian outback about 20° south.

## Wind patterns

In some parts of the world there are predictable wind patterns: at low latitudes (under about 30°) what are known as the trade winds blow towards the equator from the north-east in the northern hemisphere and the south-east in the southern; between about 30° and 60° there are prevailing westerlies, then towards the pole the norm reverts to easterly again. There are also predictable periods of calm: within about 5° north and south of the equator, two bands of wind meet and produce what are known as the Doldrums. Around 30° are the horse latitudes, another area of calm. Where these different zones converge, there tends to be unpredictable, often stormy weather.

## Ocean currents

… are another contributing factor to climate and weather. In the same way that winds try to equalize areas of different temperature and pressure, so the currents of the oceans try to do the same. Perhaps the best-known ocean current is the Gulf Stream, which flows from the Gulf of Mexico into the North Atlantic and brings warm water – and with it mild weather –up the west coast of Europe and the British Isles. Like the winds, the oceans are subject to convection currents, so in fact the Gulf Stream is only part of a cycle that brings cold water from the Arctic along the ocean floor towards the equator, where it warms, rises and flows back north again.

Also frequently in the news is El Niño, Spanish for 'the baby boy', meaning Jesus, because the phenomenon often occurs just before Christmas. Every few years this warm current, along the west coast of South America, flows particularly strongly, raising both air and ocean temperatures by 5°C or more and bringing with it heavy rain. This can be beneficial to life on land, but the warmer seawater is fatal to vast quantities of phytoplankton at the bottom end of the maritime food chain, with disastrous knock-on effects for the fish and anything that feeds on it.

The reverse effect, when air pressure is high over the eastern Pacific and low over the western Pacific, is often referred to as La Niña, 'baby girl'. For real kudos at dinner parties you could throw in the fact that both form part of a continuing seesaw pattern across the ocean known as the Southern Oscillation or ENSO (El Niño Southern Oscillation) for short.

## Rainfall

It isn't just convection currents that lead to rain or snow. Warm, moist air also has to rise when it comes up against a mountain range. The effect is the same, though: once it rises, it cools, becomes less able to retain its moisture content and is forced to let this fall on the ground below. So rain falls on the coastal side of a mountain range, leaving a dry area known as a 'rain shadow' on the other side. This phenomenon, known as **relief** or **orographic rain**, is the reason that cities such as Vancouver and Seattle, to the west (seaward side) of the Rockies, receive so much more rain than the prairies to the east, and why Big Island in Hawaii is so extraordinary. It is home to Mauna Kea, the world's tallest mountain if you measure it from the earth's crust under the sea and ignore all the water. On one side, the town of Hilo is reputed to be the wettest city in the USA: rain falls nearly every day, producing an impressive total of over 3,000 mm a year, comparable to some parts of the Amazon rainforest (notoriously wet Seattle gets 1,000 and London less than 750). On the other side of the mountain is an area where low rainfall combines with other factors such as volcanic ash and permeable soil to form a desert. Other 'rain shadow' areas include the Atacama desert of Chile, the Mojave desert in the USA and much of Tibet.

## Fronts

Rain will also occur at a **front** – that is, an imaginary line where two masses of air of different temperatures meet. The colder air sinks, pushing the warmer upward, where again water vapour condenses to form rain. Warm fronts occur when warm air is moving faster than colder, denser air and is forced up; cold fronts occur when cold air catches up with warmer air, again forcing it up. We'll not get into occluded fronts and depressions and the like because, frankly, they make for depressing weather and depressing reading. Let's just say that fronts are common in the mid-latitudes, where they give the British plenty to talk about.

# LONGITUDE AND TIME ZONES

The earth, as we know, spins on its axis every twenty-four hours, so that at any given moment the sun is directly overhead – it is midday – somewhere. As the earth keeps on spinning, that point moves out of the direct path of the sun's rays, into afternoon and night, while the next bit along comes into the light.

To help us pin this down we have a system of measurement called longitude, defined as the distance in degrees east or west of the prime meridian at 0°. The prime meridian, like all lines of longitude, runs from the North to the South Pole, while lines of latitude run round the earth, always at the same distance from the poles. It is the technical term for what most of us call Greenwich. (The techies also now call Greenwich Mean Time UTC, which they maintain is short for Co-ordinated Universal Time. The abbreviation is a compromise between the French and the English versions, with the happy result that it is confusing in both languages. So let's ignore it.)

If you have been to Greenwich in south London you will know that you can stand with your feet on either side of a metal strip and claim to be in both western and eastern hemispheres at the same time. The furthest you can get from Greenwich is 180° east or west, a point called the International Date Line. Add the 180° you have gone to get there to the 180° you will have to go to get back where you started and you have 360°, a full circle.

## So how do time zones work?

The earth's 360° of longitude are divided into twenty-four segments called hours, so that 15° (360 ÷ 24) represents an hour of time change. Anything that is, for example, 75° to the west of Greenwich will be five hours behind. As it happens, Boston is 71° west of Greenwich, New York 73° and Washington 77°, but it would clearly be daft to say that when it is noon in Greenwich it is 6.44 in Boston, 6.52 in New York and 7.08 in Washington. Instead, a 'time zone' known as Eastern Standard Time decrees that it is 7 a.m. in all three cities. This ruling applies to the US as far west as Michigan and Alabama, and most of New Brunswick, Quebec, Ontario and Nunavut in Canada – a large chunk of land.

The mainland US has four time zones: Eastern, Central, Mountain and Pacific, each differing by an hour. Thus when it is noon in New York, it is 11 a.m. in Chicago, 10 a.m. in Denver and 9 a.m. in Los Angeles. (It's also 8 a.m. in Alaska and 7 a.m in Hawaii.) It means that if you live in Michigan and your parents live in Wisconsin you probably have to change your watch every time you go for Sunday lunch, but that inconveniences fewer people than having a sixteen-minute time difference between New York and Washington.

Similarly, if you move east from the UK, you find that when it is noon in Greenwich it is 1 p.m. in Paris, 2 p.m. in Istanbul, 3 in Addis Ababa, 4 in Moscow, 5 in Islamabad and so on. (Actually not really 'and so on', because it is 5.30 in New Delhi and there are half-hour subdivisions in Australia too, but you get the picture.)

If you travel east across the Pacific and cross the International Date Line you 'gain' a day, because you pass from a zone that is twelve hours ahead of Greenwich to one that is twelve hours behind. For example, if it is 6 p.m. on Tuesday in Greenwich, crossing the International Date Line you go from 6 a.m. on Wednesday (twelve hours ahead) to 6 a.m. on Tuesday (twelve hours behind) and have to go through Tuesday all over again. Going west, you would move from 6 a.m. on Tuesday to 6 a.m. on Wednesday, having missed most of Tuesday altogether.

## There's a reason for these time zones ...

If you've read Jules Verne's *Around the World in Eighty Days*, you may remember that the hero, Phileas Fogg, ignored this newfangled (as it was in his day) system of time zones, went all the way round the globe on UK time and arrived back in London twenty-four hours earlier than he realized. Good for him, because it meant he won his bet, but for much of the trip he must have been having lunch at supper time and going to bed just when other people were thinking of getting up. The point about adjusting our watches to the rotation of the earth is that it means for most of us, most of the time, unless we live near one of the poles, it is generally light when we are up and about and dark when we want to sleep – and our bodies prefer it that way. Ask anyone who works a night shift.

# THE MAKE-UP OF THE EARTH

Current thinking is that the earth has a radius of about 6,371 km. Those in the know work this out through the study of seismic waves (that's activity associated with earthquakes), volcanic eruptions, gas escaping from the earth and so on. At the centre of the earth is the **core**, made of nickel and iron. The inner core, about 1,250 km thick, is solid; the outer core, 2,200 km thick, is permanently molten. The reason the inner core is not molten is that although the temperature of the inner core can reach 3,700°C, hot enough to melt most things, the pressure is even more powerful, keeping the metal in a solid state.

Above the core lies the **mantle**, 2,900 km thick. Some of this is solid, some of it viscous and all of it scarily hot (up to 3,000°C). Scientists divide the outer part of the mantle into two parts, the inner **asthenosphere** and the outer **lithosphere**. The lithosphere also includes the earth's **crust** – a surface layer varying between about 6 km and 70 km thick, with the thinner bits under the ocean and the thicker under the land. It's in this lithosphere that the activity which causes earthquakes and volcanic eruptions goes on.

## Plate tectonics

We know – or are pretty sure we know, but this is an area where new theories abound – that the continents were not always where they are now. Once upon a time there was a single land mass called Pangaea ('all the earth'). Back in the mists of time this split into a great northern continent known as Laurasia and a great southern one, Gondwanaland. These in turn split and drifted apart to form the continents we know today. This happened because the earth's surface is not a single smooth shell but a series of interconnecting and constantly moving plates. These plates move about over the ebb and flow of the mantle, and inevitably bump into each other.

### Rubbing along

At the edges of the plates, therefore, are areas of unrest where one plate may rub alongside another. Alternatively, one plate may be pushed under another – a process called **subduction**. This is more common with oceanic plates, when a deep ocean trench is formed, but if it happens with one or more continental plates, the result can be spectacular: scientists reckon that about 40 or 50 million years ago the plate carrying India bashed into the plate carrying the rest of Asia and pushed an enormous amount of rock upwards, forming the Himalayas. If you consider that the Himalayan range is about 2,400 km long, anything from 150 km to 400 km wide and contains fourteen mountains above 8,000 metres high, you'll appreciate that 'an enormous amount of rock' is something of an understatement.

### Divergence

The third thing that can happen to plates is that they move away from each other – **divergence**. Like subduction, this is more common under the sea than on land, but there is a classic land-based example: the Great Rift Valley in East Africa. As a result of two plates diverging, the eastern parts of Kenya and Ethiopia and all of Somalia are likely one day to split off from the rest of the continent. This is, however, unlikely to be in your lifetime or mine, so even if you are living in Somalia you needn't lose too much sleep over it.

## Earthquakes, landslides and tsunamis

Whatever the nature of the conflict between two plates, the edges are where earthquakes occur. Pressure builds up underneath the plates so that they lurch about. The lurching can be quite gentle – noticed only by sensitive instruments and, some say, dogs – or massively destructive, demolishing whole cities and killing tens of thousands of people. The amount of destruction obviously depends on the strength of the earthquake but also on where the **epicentre** is: this is the point on the earth's surface directly above the focus of the quake, where the tremors are at their strongest.

The quaking of the earth and collapse of buildings are not the only effects of earthquakes. Landslides and tsunamis (see below) cause further and often greater destruction. The devastating tsunami of December 2004 occurred as a direct result of an undersea earthquake off the island of Sumatra. Admittedly it was one of the largest earthquakes ever recorded, but it was the tsunami that produced a death toll close to 250,000 people.

**What is a tsunami?**

It's the proper name for what used inaccurately to be called a tidal wave. A tsunami is a massive sea wave created by seismic activity – usually an earthquake or volcanic eruption – under the ocean. The worst waves of the 2004 tsunami reached a height of a terrifying 30 metres. That, in case you have trouble visualizing it, is about the height of a nine-storey building.

## Volcanoes

There are a number of different kinds, but the classic ones are conical in shape (Japan's iconic Mount Fuji is a near-perfect example). They are formed from molten rocks and other debris that has been flung out of the earth. The inside of a volcano is a funnel that goes down deep enough into the earth to reach that molten stuff and provide an outlet when it needs to burst out.

Let's go back to the movement of those plates. Where there are gaps between them or the rocks are thinner than normal, the superheated molten rock beneath – magma – wells up to fill the gaps or to create what is known as a **hot spot** on the earth's crust. When pressure builds up beneath it – as it does, just take my word for it – it erupts. Because magma (which becomes known as lava once it has reached the earth's surface) is not always the same consistency or chemical composition, it can erupt in different ways, flinging out gas and ash as well as rocks.

## Mountains and rocks

So volcanoes are one sort of mountain and those formed by land masses crashing into each other are another. The land-masses-crashing type come in various forms, of which the most common is the **fold mountain**, caused when two continental plates hit each other and the earth's crust is uplifted, forming folds one on top of the other. Most of the world's great mountains ranges – including the Himalayas, the Andes, the Rockies and the European Alps – come into this category.

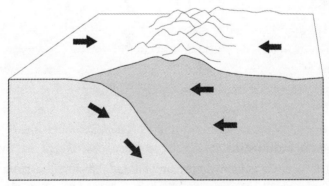

Two continental plates
hit each other and uplift
the earth's crust

Rocks and land masses are not perfect and uniform throughout. There are often faults or fracture lines through them. These can range from massive faults that are found where tectonic plates rub along each other (see **Rubbing along** on page 148) to smaller fractures that cause blocks of rock to shift around. Sometimes these are quite small; sometimes they are big enough to form **fault-block mountains**. Material from below is forced upwards and other material collapses, often forming a rift valley. With the mountains, you end up with one sheer side and one sloping one. Examples are seen in the Rhine Valley and in the Sierra Nevada in California.

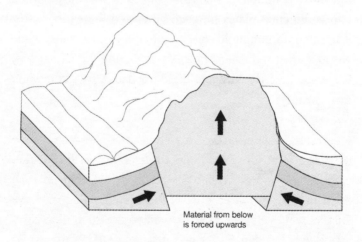

Material from below
is forced upwards

**Dome mountains** are similar to volcanoes, except that the magma never actually bursts out: instead it pushes the earth's crust upwards. Because less force is involved than with fold mountains, dome mountains don't tend to be as high: the Black Hills of Dakota, often quoted as an example, barely top 2,200 metres, whereas even the European Alps (tiny in comparison to the Himalayas and the Andes on the fold-mountain list) get to 4,800 metres.

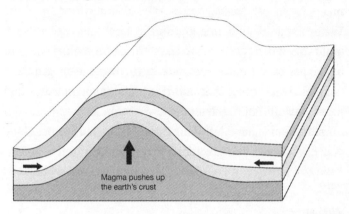

Magma pushes up
the earth's crust

Whatever type of mountain you are dealing with, erosion comes into play the moment it is born. Over a period of millions of years, weathering will wash away softer rock to leave a harder core, soften the contours and even allow soil to develop and grass to grow. So as a rule of thumb, the pointier, craggier and more barren a mountain is, the younger it is. Even the gently rolling hills of the southern English Lake District were volcanic once – but that was 460 million years ago. Maybe in another 400 million years or so the Himalayas will be no more challenging to walk in than Cumbria.

## The sculptors of geography
Plate movement isn't the only factor that shapes the earth. The other absolutely crucial one is water, whether in liquid or frozen form. As you'll know if you've ever been caught

unawares by a wave when swimming in the sea, water is powerful stuff. Perhaps more surprisingly, so is ice.

## Ice

Water expands as it freezes, and in large quantities it can build up enough pressure to move or carve rock. The earth has experienced many ice ages in its time, when **glaciers** – large 'rivers' of ice that start in a high mountain valley and move downhill until the temperature becomes warm enough to melt them – have left their mark on the landscape. Once you know what you are looking for, you can tell a glacial valley at a glance: it is usually U-shaped in cross-section.

## Water

Water itself can beat away at a coastline or land formation, producing headlands, spits, arches and caves. There is no rule that says any area needs to be made up of only one kind of rock, and water will – over lots of time, remember – worm its way through the softer variety, sometimes leaving remarkable results. A spectacular example can be seen at Victoria Falls in southern Africa, where the waters of the Zambezi river plummet down a 100-metre drop formed millions of years ago by volcanic activity. This covered the area with basalt, which, as it cooled, cracked to leave massive fissures that eventually filled with limestone. Limestone is much softer than basalt, and the water has forced its way through, in an ever-repeating cycle of eroding one section of the falls and creating another. The present falls are perhaps 100 km south of where they were 100 million years ago and edging their way slowly upriver towards the Zambezi's source in Angola.

## CLOUDS

Cloud fanciers identify innumerable different types of cloud, with subdivisions such as *Cumulus mediocris* and *Stratocumulus castellanus* but, as you can see from the list below, to have a back-to-basics handle on clouds you need to memorize just five words and put them together in combination:

- **Alto** is the easy one: it's from the Latin for high. You'll notice that altocumulus is higher than ordinary cumulus. It's all you need to know.

- **Cirrus** are the thin wisps of cloud very high up in the sky. They don't produce rain but are often an indication that bad weather is on its way.

- **Cumulus** are the white fluffy ones that those of us who can't draw produce when we try to draw clouds. They're the ones you see on pleasant, partly cloudy days.

- **Nimbus** doesn't occur on its own: it's either **cumulonimbus**, the big fluffy storm clouds that are associated with rain, lightning and thunder; or **nimbostratus**, the stormy, rainy version of stratus.

- **Stratus** are flat, uniform, greyish clouds often seeming to cover the whole sky. They don't produce much rain, but may drizzle.

So put them all together and what have you got? Starting from the ground, the ten most common types of cloud and their approximate altitudes are:

**Stratus** (below 1,500 metres)
**Cumulus** (between 1,000 and 3,000 metres)
**Cumulonimbus** (between 1,000 and 12,000 metres)
**Stratocumulus** (between 1,500 and 3,000 metres)
**Nimbostratus** (between 1,500 and 3,000 metres)
**Altostratus** (between 4,500 and 6,000 metres)
**Altocumulus** (around 6,000 metres)
**Cirrostratus** (between 7,500 and 9,000 metres)
**Cirrocumulus** (between 9,000 and 11,000 metres)
**Cirrus** (around 12,000 metres)

## A GEOGRAPHY GLOSSARY

Perhaps more than any other subject, geography has a vocabulary that non-geographers feel they ought to understand. Somehow no non-scientist is embarrassed about being rubbish at science, but geography crosses that inscrutable barrier into 'general knowledge' that makes ignorance uncomfortable. So here is a list of a few expressions we have all almost certainly heard …

**Antipodes:** used loosely simply to mean 'Australia and New Zealand', this is strictly a plural, meaning a pair of points on opposite sides of the globe. So the antipode of where you are now is the place you'd get to if you started digging and kept going straight until you came out the other side. (In theory, that is – please don't try it at home.) The actual antipode of London is close to the island group known, surprisingly enough, as the Antipodes, about 860 km south-east of the southernmost part of New Zealand.

**Archipelago:** any chain or group of islands. Many of the nation-states of Oceania are archipelagos: Indonesia is made up of about 13,000 islands, the Philippines 7,000 and even little Tonga over 150.

**Atoll:** a ring of coral forming an island or group of islands in the sea. The Bikini Atoll used to be the most famous – in the 1940s and 1950s the US experimented with 'nuclear devices' there and a French designer named a swimsuit after it. Nowadays people tend to have heard of the Maldives too.

**Caldera:** from the Latin for cooking pot, a large volcanic crater usually formed by the collapse of the volcano following an eruption, and often many times larger than the original vent. The Ngorongoro Crater in Tanzania, a great wildlife tourist attraction, is an ancient caldera, over 600 metres deep and covering an area of more than 250 square kilometres.

**Ice age:** a very extended cold snap. During the last one, around 10,000 years ago, about a third of the earth's surface was covered by ice. We are now in an **interglacial period**, which means that we are waiting for the next ice age to come along.

**Igneous rock:** formed when molten lava or magma solidifies at or beneath the earth's surface.

**Isthmus:** a neck of land connecting two larger land masses. The Isthmus of Panama, for example, is the narrow strip joining North and South America.

**Lagoon:** a body of seawater that is almost completely cut off from the ocean by a barrier beach or a coral reef. The world's largest is Grand Lagon Sud (which means 'big southern lake') in New Caledonia, covering an area of about 24,000 square kilometres.

**Meander:** a bend in a river caused by faster-flowing water on one side cutting away one bank while slower-flowing water on the other side drops material and builds up the other bank. This normally happens in the middle or lower course of a river, when it is flowing over flat land.

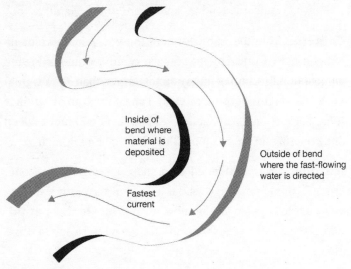

Inside of bend where material is deposited

Outside of bend where the fast-flowing water is directed

Fastest current

**Metamorphic rock:** rock that has changed as a result of prolonged pressure and heat. Slate, for example, is shale that has been transformed into slabs, while marble is a limestone that has been heated and crushed until it recrystallizes as a different, far harder rock.

**Oxbow lake:** if you are ever lucky enough to fly over the Mississippi River on a clear day, you'll see more meanders and oxbow lakes than you ever thought possible – it may arouse an interest in geography you never knew you possessed. An oxbow is created when a meander (see opposite) becomes so pronounced that its two ends find themselves close to each other. Then, usually during a time of high, fast-flowing water, the main river takes the easiest and quickest course and cuts across the 'neck' of the meander, cutting off the rest of the curve. Where the water slows, it deposits what geographers call 'load' on either side of the channel, leaving a crescent-shaped or oxbow lake. This may eventually dry out and leave, almost literally, only a shadow of its former self.

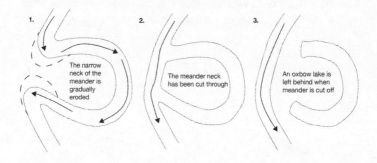

**Peninsula:** from the Latin 'almost an island', a piece of land that sticks out into a body of water. Most of Florida is one, as is most of Italy.

**Sedimentary rock:** layers of rock or other material that build up on the floor of a river or ocean. They have generally started out as sand, gravel, etc., washed down from a mountain through erosion or, in the case of limestone, as tiny organisms living in a warm shallow sea. Over time these layers are compacted or squashed down and form rock. Then when rivers change their course, oceans retreat over time, or faults or tectonic activity move these rocks about, they reappear on the surface. Sandstone, shale and limestone are three of the most familiar types of sedimentary rock.

**Strait:** a narrow body of water connecting two larger ones, and separating two islands or land masses. Cook Strait, for example, separates the North and South Islands of New Zealand and runs between the Tasman Sea and the South Pacific.

**Tributary:** a river or stream flowing into a larger one: the Madeira, the Purus and the Yapura, all major rivers in their own right, are nevertheless tributaries of the Amazon.

# GENERAL STUDIES

This is the catch-all subject that lets us keep up with art, music, religion and various other bits and pieces that don't fit in anywhere else. Because it's general, it includes all sorts of things we all know a bit about – and are perhaps embarrassed not to know more.

## MUSIC ...

Let's start with music.

### Some musical terms

Some of these have crossed over into non-musical speech, most notably the much-abused *crescendo* (which, contrary to popular belief, is *not* a loud thing but rather the process of becoming louder). In fact these terms are almost all day-to-day Italian words giving instructions about speed and volume.

**Adagio:** slow – slower than *andante* but not as slow as *largo*. Often used to describe the slow movement of a symphony, concerto, etc.

**Allegro:** cheerful, quick, bright. *Allegretto* is not quite as cheerful, but still pretty perky.

**Andante:** slow – literally 'at a walking pace'.

**Brio:** spirit, vigour, so *con brio*: vigorously.

**Cantabile:** 'singingly', i.e. smoothly and with the melody well brought out.

**Crescendo:** becoming gradually louder.

**Diminuendo:** becoming gradually quieter.

**Forte (f):** loud. *Fortissimo (ff)*: very loud; you occasionally also see *fff*, which may mean you need to nail the roof back on once it's over.

**Largo:** broad, i.e. slow and dignified.

**Lento:** slow.

**Mezzo:** half, quite, as in *mezzo forte (mf)*, quite loud, or *mezzo piano (mp)*, quite soft.

**Moderato:** moderate, at a moderate pace.

**Piano (p):** quiet, soft. *Pianissimo (pp)*: even quieter, and *pianississimo (ppp)*, hardly worth getting the instrument out of its case.

**Pizzicato:** plucked, used when the instruction is to pluck the strings of, for example, a violin, instead of using the bow.

**Presto:** quick. *Prestissimo* is even quicker.

**Scherzo:** playful; either an individual piece or the most cheerful movement of a symphony, etc.

**Staccato:** literally 'detached', indicated by a dot over the note and meaning 'let go of the note rather than holding it down for its full value'. Hence the more general meaning of 'short, clipped', as in staccato speech or staccato sounds.

**Vivace:** lively.

## Musical forms

**Chamber music:** this is a term used loosely to describe anything that does not involve a solo instrument (either alone or accompanied by another instrument) on the one hand or a full orchestra or choir on the other. Much of chamber music is written for a string quartet – normally two violins, a viola and a cello – but it can also include duet sonatas, trios or anything up to an octet.

**Concerto:** a work, often in three movements, featuring a solo instrument backed by an orchestra. Famous ones include Rachmaninov's for the piano (no. 2 being the tear-jerking theme for the film *Brief Encounter*), Elgar's for the cello and Saint-Saëns' for the organ.

**Fugue:** a work for a number of parts or voices, in which each enters in turn, imitating the previous one.

**Movement:** a self-contained section of a larger piece such as a symphony, concerto or sonata, usually with its own tempo. Beethoven's Fifth Symphony, for example, is in four movements, designated *allegro con brio*, *andante con moto*, *scherzo* and *allegro*.

**Sonata:** a work, generally in three movements, for piano only, or for piano and one other instrument. The greatest are by Haydn, Mozart and Beethoven (notably the Pathétique), though most twentieth-century composers have written them too. A **sonatina** is a shorter, usually lighter form.

**Symphony:** a large-scale work for full orchestra, usually in four movements. The *Oxford Dictionary of Music* says that the form is 'reserved by composers for their most weighty and profound musical thoughts, but of course there are many light-hearted, witty and entertaining symphonies'. Among the most famous are Beethoven's Fifth (da da da daaa!) and Ninth (the Choral Symphony), Schubert's Eighth (the Unfinished) and Mahler's Ninth.

## The orchestra

The instruments of the orchestra are divided into four sections:

- **Strings**: violin, viola, cello, double bass.

- **Woodwind**: oboe, cor anglais, flute, piccolo, clarinet, bassoon.

- **Brass**: trumpet, trombone, tuba, horn.

- **Percussion**: drums, timpani, cymbals and other occasionally used instruments such as the xylophone, glockenspiel and celesta.

Who sits where is established by convention – the strings in the front, with the violins to the conductor's left, the violas straight in front of him and the cellos and double basses to his right, the woodwinds behind the violas, and so on, as shown in the illustration.

The harp doesn't appear very often in a symphony orchestra; when it does it sits alongside the percussion, although pedants maintain that it is a stringed instrument. Any fool could tell that by looking at it, of course, but the pedantic point is that the word *percussion* comes from the Latin for 'to hit' and that the harp is plucked rather than struck. You may feel that life

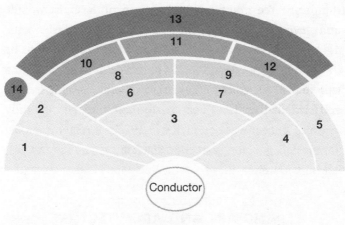

Conductor

**Strings**
1. First violins
2. Second violins
3. Violas
4. Cellos
5. Double basses

**Woodwind**
6. Flutes
7. Oboes
8. Clarinets
9. Bassoons

**Brass**
10. Horns
11. Trumpets
12. Trombones
    and tuba

**Percussion and harp**
13. Timpani and other percussion instruments
14. Harp

is too short for this to matter, but there is a lot of discussion about it on the internet.

A symphony orchestra normally consists of ninety or more instruments, the exact number and breakdown of them depending on the music being played. Sticking to Beethoven's Fifth for our model, it is scored for piccolo, two flutes, two oboes, two clarinets, two bassoons, contrabassoon, two horns, two trumpets, three trombones, timpani and strings; Mahler's Ninth, on the other hand, requires piccolo, four flutes, three oboes, cor anglais, five clarinets, four bassoons (fourth doubling contrabassoon), four French horns, three trumpets, three trombones, tuba, timpani, bass drum, side drum, cymbals, triangle, tambourine, tam-tam, three bells, glockenspiel, two harps and strings. You surely have to be very grown up not to add 'and a partridge in a pear tree' to a list like that. As for Havergal Brian's Gothic Symphony, it's so enormous that it has been performed in its entirety only six times since it was completed in 1927 – it requires almost 200 musicians before you even start on the choirs (and yes, that is *choirs* plural).

## ... AND ART AND ARCHITECTURE

Here's a chance to brush up on some general, but nevertheless useful, artistic terms that you might have encountered before.

Classical, romantic, baroque, rococo – we've heard the words, applied sometimes to music, sometimes to other aspects of the arts. But how happy would any of us be about putting up our hands and explaining what they mean? Let's have a go.

Starting with the earliest, the **baroque** period lasted from around 1600 to 1750 and in music its most famous proponents were Johann Sebastian Bach, Handel and Vivaldi. The term was borrowed from the decorative German and Austrian architecture of the period and used to describe the more complex harmonies that these composers were developing: music, like architecture, was becoming more ornate.

**Rococo** is a spin-off of baroque, used more in the visual arts than in music. That said, people will be impressed if you apply it to the works of Johann Christian Bach, one of the numerous sons of the more famous Johann Sebastian. Graceful, light but elaborate ornament is the order of the day here. The architectural style, immensely popular on the Continent, never really caught on in Britain, perhaps because we thought it was a bit French. For the best examples you need to go to the Charlottenburg Palace in Berlin or look out for any furniture described as Louis XV.

**Classical** is hard to define because we use it in so many ways. Strictly speaking, it means 'to do with Ancient Greece or Rome', so that classical literature is written by Sophocles or Virgil, but not by Shakespeare or Dickens. Classical architecture is solidly built with columns in the front (and when this style was revived in the eighteenth century it was called neo-classicism). But we tend to apply the term loosely to anything that has stood the test of time, regardless of style: a musician would say that Schumann and Chopin wrote romantic music, but a non-expert might lump them in with Beethoven and Mozart and say that it was all 'classical' because it was nearly two hundred years old, not likely to go out of fashion, and noticeably different from jazz, rock or pop.

Classical music, though, strictly refers to the period 1750–1830, when the symphony and the concerto were being developed, and when Haydn, Mozart and Beethoven were writing.

Last of the four was the **romantic** period. Romantic music tends to date from about 1830 to 1900 and in addition to Schumann and Chopin might have been composed by Schubert, Berlioz, Wagner or Liszt. The defining element is that emotional and picturesque expression is more important than structure or form, an idea that would have been anathema to Bach or Haydn. The romantic composers were inspired by the slightly earlier romantic movement in literature, whose principal writers were Coleridge, Wordsworth, Keats, Byron, Shelley and, on the Continent, Hugo and Goethe. Their works were concerned with the emotions and with our responses to nature; they were in part a reaction against the eighteenth-century Age of Reason, known in France as the Enlightenment, when everything had to be explained rather than felt (see page 95 for more on this).

## Architecture

Going back to classical architecture and all those columns, there are three principal styles or **orders** and they are mostly differentiated by the amount of decoration they have on the capital (the bit at the top of the column, before you get to the entablature, which is the bit it is holding up).

- **Doric:** the oldest and the plainest, sturdy and with no adornment. There are plenty of them on the Parthenon in Athens.

- **Ionic:** slimmer and with four spiral scrolls at the top, as seen in the Banqueting House in Whitehall in London, or in the typical Antebellum house of the American South.

- **Corinthian:** much fancier. The top is decorated with the leaves of the plant *Acanthus mollis* or bear's breeches. Examples are to be found in the Pantheon in Rome and in the Capitol in Washington DC.

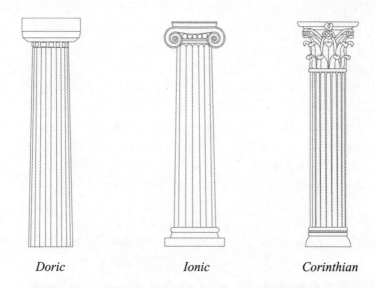

*Doric*          *Ionic*          *Corinthian*

While we're looking at old buildings, it's worth adding a few more styles of architecture, as embodied in the shapes of the arches and the windows.

- **Norman** (in Britain) or **Romanesque** (in the rest of Europe, about the sixth to the twelfth centuries): characterized by a simple semicircular arch but also including the great square towers that are typical of castles and cathedrals of the period. The White Tower in the Tower of London, and many of the great English cathedrals, including Canterbury, Durham and Ely, are Romanesque, as is the abbey at Mont St-Michel in France.

*This illustration shows the semi-circular arches typical of Norman architecture*

● **Gothic:** the arches are narrow and pointed at the top, and were the common style across northern Europe from about the twelfth to the sixteenth centuries. Grand buildings of the period also feature flying buttresses (see page 172) and rose windows: Notre-Dame de Paris and Chartres

*A close-up view of a Gothic arch and a rose window*

Cathedral are prime examples. The eighteenth and nineteenth centuries produced a movement called the Gothic Revival, epitomized by the London Houses of Parliament.

**Palladian:** named after the Italian architect Antonio Palladio (1508–80) and characterized by a return to the symmetry of Greek and Roman temples, harmonious proportions, semicircular arches over the windows and lots of columns. One of Palladio's most important disciples was the Englishman Inigo Jones (1573–1652), who reproduced this style in the Banqueting Hall in Whitehall and in St Paul's Church, Covent Garden. Thomas Jefferson also followed Palladio's principles when he designed his home at Monticello.

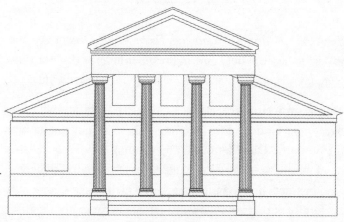

*An example of Palladian architecture*

**What exactly is a flying buttress?**

You know what they look like – you've seen them at York Minster or Notre-Dame – but what are they for?

Well, a buttress is a mass of masonry built against or projecting from a wall to strengthen or support it. The flying version is one of the great innovations of Gothic architecture: in addition to the traditional chunky buttress, it has a 'flyer' or partial arch that helps to resist the outward thrust or pressure of the building. It is also load-bearing, which means that walls can be thinner and/or that more space can be allowed for non-load-bearing features such as windows. So the development of the flying buttress went hand in hand with the increased use of stained glass in medieval cathedrals.

# THE BIBLE

Seen *Joseph and the Amazing Technicolor Dreamcoat*, but just a bit vague about some of the other famous Bible stories? Here are just a few that we have all heard a little about.

**Noah and the ark** (Genesis 6–9): people are behaving badly and God decides to punish them (a not uncommon theme in the Old Testament) by sending a flood to destroy them. Noah, however, is excluded from the general slaughter: God instructs him to build an ark in which to shelter not only his family but also a male and a female of 'every living thing of all flesh' to keep them alive. Noah obeys; it then rains for forty days and forty nights and all the corrupt and evil people are drowned. Noah eventually sends out a dove to see if the floodwaters have receded and she returns with an olive leaf in her mouth – hence the symbolism of both a dove and an olive branch as signs of peace. God also sends a rainbow as his promise to Noah that this will never happen again (though he does continue to exhibit his power and his wrath in other ways).

**Joseph** (Genesis 37–45): he is Jacob's favourite among his twelve sons. He (Jacob) gives him (Joseph) a coat of many colours that makes his brothers sick with envy. They sell him to some traders who in turn sell him into slavery in Egypt. But Joseph is bright, has God on his side and is able to interpret Pharaoh's troubling dreams, so that in due course he becomes Pharaoh's right-hand man, saves Egypt from famine and is even able to be magnanimous to his brothers when the time comes. Jacob is also known as Israel (which means 'power with God') and his twelve sons become the fathers of the twelve tribes of Israel, aka the Children of Israel – the Jews.

**Moses** (most of the book of Exodus): he leads the Children of Israel out of Egypt, where they have been enslaved under a later Pharaoh who isn't as benevolent as Joseph's one. Moses – called upon by God during a much-reported encounter with a burning bush – asks Pharaoh to 'let my people go'; Pharaoh refuses and God sends various plagues (of frogs, locusts and the like) to encourage him to change his mind. The last plague entails smiting the firstborn of Egypt: everyone's eldest child is to be killed, but the Children of Israel are to smear their houses with the blood of a lamb they have eaten and God will 'pass over' these houses and spare the offspring. God also instructs Moses to celebrate this 'passover' for ever more. After this massacre, Pharaoh relents and the Israelites go on their way. Pharaoh then promptly changes his mind, sets off in pursuit and God parts the waters of the sea so that the Israelites can cross in safety. When the Egyptians try to follow, they are inevitably drowned *en masse*.

The Israelites then spend forty years in the desert, during which Moses climbs Mount Sinai and receives the Ten Commandments from God, before they are finally allowed to enter the Promised Land of Canaan (modern Israel and surrounds). In punishment for some failing that isn't clear, Moses himself is allowed to see the Promised Land, but not enter it. He dies at the age of 120, making him a mere child in Old Testament terms (Noah lives to be 950 and his grandfather Methuselah notches up 969 years).

**Samson and Delilah** (Judges 13–16): in the Old Testament the Philistines are neighbours of the Israelites, with whom they are frequently involved in skirmishes. Samson, one of the judges (in this context a hero or military leader) of Israel, is a man of enormous strength and a short fuse: he kills thirty men because they find out the answer to a riddle by cheating, so is not someone you want to cross. The Philistines, eager to get their hands on him, persuade Samson's lover Delilah to wheedle out of him the secret of his great strength. Poor man: the Bible actually says, 'She pressed him daily with her words, and urged him, so that his soul was vexed unto death.' There must be a lot of men who know how he felt. Anyway, he finally confesses that his long hair is the secret; Delilah cuts it off while he is asleep and the Philistines are able to rush in, blind him and put him in prison. He languishes there for a while and – you would think the Philistines might have thought of this – his hair grows back. So that when he is brought out to be ridiculed during a festival, he is strong enough to pull down the pillars of the house and crush 3,000 people. Did I say he wasn't a man to cross?

**David and Goliath** (1 Samuel 17): Goliath is another Philistine and also a giant: six cubits and a span, the Bible tells us – about 3 metres. He is terrorizing the Israelites, challenging them to send a man to fight him in single combat. David, a young shepherd boy, goes to King Saul and volunteers; despite much scoffing he fells Goliath with a stone from his slingshot, which hits the giant on the forehead and knocks him cold long enough for David to cut his head off. David subsequently becomes the close friend of Saul's son, Jonathan (their names are still a byword for inseparable buddies). He also marries Saul's daughter, so that when Saul and Jonathan are killed in battle it is reasonable for David to become king. Among his children are Absalom, who rebels against him and is killed after his head is caught in the branches of a tree, and Solomon, proverbial for his wisdom. Through Solomon, David becomes a forefather of Jesus – the first chapter of Matthew's gospel give the genealogy of who begat whom through the many intervening generations.

**Daniel:** he is important enough to have a book to himself and it has a number of famous tales in it. By now the Israelites' main enemies are the Babylonians, whose king is

Nebuchadnezzar. Daniel and his friends Shadrach, Meshach and Abednego are taken into exile in Babylon (in modern Iraq), where Daniel's wisdom and ability to interpret the king's dreams (clearly a useful Old Testament skill) make him a favoured person at court. But Nebuchadnezzar is furious when Shadrach, Meshach and Abednego insist on worshipping their own God; he throws them, tied up, into a fiery furnace, where they are soon seen walking about free and unburnt.

Nebuchadnezzar is succeeded by his son Belshazzar, he of the famous feast at which a man's fingers appear out of nowhere and write on the wall. Daniel is again summoned to interpret and he reads the words, '*Mene, mene, tekel, upharsin*'. These are usually interpreted as 'Thou art weighed in the balance and art found wanting', but in fact also include the warning that God has put an end to the kingdom, divided it and given it to the Medes and Persians. It's a punishment for Belshazzar's arrogance: he dies that night and is succeeded by Darius the Mede.

Other prominent men now plot against Daniel, with the result that his praying to God becomes a crime punishable by being thrown into the lions' den. But again, God is on his side and he emerges safe and sound. His enemies are unmasked and are themselves thrown to the lions, who thereby get their dinner after all.

**The Good Samaritan** (Luke 10): Jesus uses many parables in the course of his preaching, a parable being a story that uses familiar events to illustrate a moral message. The Good Samaritan is perhaps the most famous of them. Jesus has been preaching about loving thy neighbour and someone asks,

'Who is my neighbour?' Well, says Jesus, 'a certain man went down from Jerusalem to Jericho and fell among thieves.' They robbed him, beat him up and left him half dead. After two people, one of them a priest, have come along the road, seen the injured man and 'passed by on the other side', a Samaritan stops and takes care of him, going to considerable trouble and expense. The fact that the Samaritans are a people that the Jews traditionally hate makes his act of 'neighbourliness' all the more significant.

## A FEW CLASSICAL MYTHS

Like the biblical stories, some of these have passed into the language. Also like the biblical stories, you could fill a book with them, so here is just a smattering.

**Helen of Troy:** she is actually the wife of Menelaus, King of Sparta, but ends up in Troy because she runs off with the Trojan prince Paris. Or she may have been abducted by him – opinions vary as to how much of it is her fault. The result is the war in which various Greek nobles, including Odysseus (Ulysses in Latin), Agamemnon and Achilles, attempt to take her back. Achilles is the greatest warrior among them, because he is all but invincible: his immortal mother dipped him in a river in the Underworld in order to make him immortal too. Unfortunately, she held him by the heel, so he is killed when an arrow strikes him in that vulnerable part – hence not only the metaphorical *Achilles' heel* but the literal *Achilles tendon* of modern English. Troy is finally taken by a trick: the Greeks build a wooden horse and offer it to the

Trojans as a gift; the Trojans take it inside their city walls, not realizing that it is full of Greek soldiers, who burst out and destroy the city. Odysseus, having already been at war for ten years, takes another ten years to find his way home. The trip is described in Homer's epic poem *The Odyssey* and has ever since given its name to any arduous journey, including one in space described by Arthur C. Clarke.

**Hercules** (known in Greek as Heracles)**:** he is a superhero or demigod, the son of Zeus by a mortal woman (Zeus was incorrigibly promiscuous and sired a lot of demigods). For complicated reasons, Hercules has to perform twelve near-impossible labours – hence the modern expression *a herculean task.* Fortunately, he is a man of huge strength and considerable resourcefulness, so he is able to kill a lion with his bare hands, capture a boar by driving it through a snowdrift, clean a stable that hasn't been mucked out for thirty years by diverting a couple of rivers through it and so on – the way you do when you are a superhero. The rest of us might have found it all a bit daunting.

**Jason:** persuaded that the golden fleece (the skin of an animal that was a gift from one of the gods, hence its goldenness) belongs in his family, Jason sets off with fifty companions to bring it back. Their ship is called the *Argo*, from which the men take the name Argonauts. The sorceress Medea, who has fallen in love with Jason, helps them achieve their task. He stays with her long enough to father two children, but then abandons her and, according to the play by Euripides, she subsequently murders her own children to get back at him.

**Midas:** a king who wishes that everything he touches will turn to gold, ignoring the fact that the gods are notoriously literally minded and interpret 'everything' as, well, *everything*. His food, his drink, his daughter ... He soon realizes the error of his ways, so it's slightly odd that today *to have the Midas touch*, meaning finding it easy to make money, should be seen as a good thing.

**Oedipus:** marries his mother Jocasta through a series of errors of judgement. The marriage, and the fact that Oedipus will kill his own father, are predicted at Oedipus's birth, so the baby is exposed on a hillside to die. He is rescued and brought up by a kindly shepherd, so that when as a grown man he returns to his home city of Thebes the prophecy is fulfilled and much misery and mayhem ensue. Many centuries later Sigmund Freud coined the term *Oedipus complex* to describe the sexual feelings that he believed children of both sexes had for their mother.

## WORDS OF WISDOM

History, literature, science and politics are all littered with people as famous for their bons mots as for their other achievements. Here are just a few that you may have happened across in the course of a lifetime of general studies. I've chosen them not because they are the author's most famous quotes but because, even out of context, they seem to have a germ of truth in them.

'As long as war is regarded as wicked, it will always have its fascination. When it is looked upon as vulgar, it will cease to be popular.'
*Irish playwright and wit Oscar Wilde in 'The Critic as Artist', 1891. Not perhaps his most famous remark, but unusual in that it is possible he was being serious*

'Adam was but human – this explains it all. He did not want the apple for the apple's sake, he wanted it only because it was forbidden.'
*American writer Mark Twain in* Pudd'nhead Wilson, *1894*

'If my theory of relativity is proven correct, Germany will claim me as a German and France will declare that I am a citizen of the world. Should my theory prove untrue, France will say that I am a German and Germany will declare that I am a Jew.'
*Physicist Albert Einstein, a German-born Jew, c. 1930*

'Dictators ride to and fro upon tigers which they dare not dismount. And the tigers are getting hungry.'
*Future British Prime Minister Winston Churchill, 1937, predicting an imminent Second World War*

'Ask not what your country can do for you – ask what you can do for your country.'
*US President John F. Kennedy in his inaugural address, 1961*

'I have a dream that my four little children will one day live in a nation where they will not be judged by the colour of their skin but by the content of their character.'

*US civil rights campaigner Martin Luther King Jr. in his most famous speech, 1963*

## NATURE STUDY

Every now and then they let you out of the classroom to roam around the grounds or the local park and you were supposed to take notice of what you saw. In case you didn't, here are some of the trees you may have come across:

**Beech** (*Fagus*): can be found throughout Europe and North America. When the leaves – ovalish with wavy edges – are on the trees they form a dense canopy, so that not much grows underneath. Beeches are often used for hedges, which retain some brown leaves throughout the winter.

**Birch** (*Betula*): the most famous species is the silver birch, whose trunks glow white-silver in winter. It's a tall, thinnish tree with hanging catkins in spring and diamond-shaped leaves.

**Cypress:** quite a few trees are lumped together under this name, the most common being the much-reviled Leylandii (x *Cuprocyparis leylandii* – the x means that it is a hybrid). It's reviled because it grows so quickly and therefore gets out of control: it's the dark, looming thing that many people have as a ridiculously tall hedge at the bottom of the garden if they *really* don't like their neighbours.

**Elm** (*Ulmus*): a rare sight in England since Dutch elm disease more or less wiped it out in the 1970s, this is still plentiful in Scotland and in eastern parts of North America. The leaves are longish but roundish with wavy edges. Different species come in different shapes, but the classic elm tree is narrow with many branches spreading neatly from the central trunk.

**Eucalyptus** (*Eucalyptus*): the famous Australian gum tree, with long, thin, grey-green leaves, peeling bark, the comforting scent of Vicks Vaporub and, if you are lucky, a koala or two asleep in the upper branches.

**Holly** (*Ilex*): this is one you probably do recognize, if only from Christmas cards – sharp, spiky, usually very dark-green leaves and bright-red berries. Just to keep you on your toes, though, there are species with pale yellow edges to the leaves, others that produce yellow or orange berries and still others that aren't prickly at all.

**Horse chestnut** (*Aesculus*): a massive tree with leaves divided into anything from five to nine lobes, best known for the conkers it produces in autumn. Depending on the species it may be covered in white or pink flowers in spring.

**Maple** (*Acer*): there are many species of all shapes and sizes, including diminutive Japanese varieties, but most have leaves divided into three or five parts, each with three points. (The one on the Canadian flag is a stylized version, but near enough to help you out.) Most maple leaves turn a glorious red in autumn and one, the paper bark maple, has bark that peels off like tissue paper. Sycamores also belong to the *Acer* family and have similar leaves.

**Oak** (*Quercus*)**:** if you are six years old and/or can't draw, this is what you produce when you try to draw a tree: a round head of leaves and branches that start quite near the ground. The leaves have rounded lobes and the 'fruits' are acorns.

**Pine** (*Pinus*)**:** the archetypal tall thin conifer which produces, surprisingly enough, pine cones.

**Poplar** (*Populus*)**:** the best-known species is noticeably tall and thin, grown in rows as windbreaks in bleak parts of East Anglia and across France and Italy, and was much painted by Monet.

**Redwood** (*Sequoia*)**:** this is the ginormous tree that you can drive through if you go to the right place in California: it genuinely does grow so big that you can cut an arch through its trunk – without the need for flying buttresses (see page 172). It's a conifer, so it has needles rather than leaves, and its wood is – well, not scarlet or crimson, but definitely reddish. But mostly what you need to know is that it is *big*.

**Rowan** (*Sorbus*): also called mountain ash, it's the one you see absolutely covered in red berries at the beginning of autumn.

**Spruce** (*Picea*): another conifer, conical in shape and with what the experts call whorled branches, which means they curve around the trunk. If the oak is everyone's idea of an everyday tree, the spruce is most people's idea of a Christmas tree.

**Willow** (*Salix*): the weeping variety is often seen along rivers, dropping mournfully towards the water – in an open space it tends to look as if it needs a haircut. The leaves are very long and thin.

**Yew** (*Taxus*): very sombre-looking conifer, lives to be very old and gnarled, grows in churchyards and is often used for formal hedges and topiary in stately homes. Don't let your kids or dog near it – almost every part of it is poisonous.

# Bibliography

Brian Cosgrove, *Weather* (Dorling Kindersley Eyewitness Guides, 1990)

John Cushnie, *Trees for the Garden* (Kyle Cathie, 2002)

Kenneth C. Davis, *Don't Know Much About Geography* (William Morrow, 1992)

Michael Kennedy, *The Oxford Dictionary of Music* (Oxford University Press, revised edition 1994)

Bruce Marshall, *The Real World* (Houghton Mifflin, 1991)

Harold Osborne (ed.), *The Oxford Companion to Art* (Oxford University Press, 1970)

Ian Ousby, *The Cambridge Guide to Literature in English* (Cambridge University Press, revised edition 1993)

*Oxford Encyclopedia of World History* (Oxford University Press, 1998)

Caroline Taggart, *A Classical Education* (Michael O'Mara, 2009)

Caroline Taggart, *Her Ladyship's Guide to the Queen's English* (National Trust, 2010)

Caroline Taggart & J. A. Wines, *My Grammar and I (or should that be 'Me'?)* (Michael O'Mara, 2008)

Marianne Taylor, *I Used To Know That: General Science* (Michael O'Mara, 2010)

Will Williams, *I Used To Know That: Geography* (Michael O'Mara, 2010)

Angela Wright, *The Beginner's Guide to Colour Psychology* (Kyle Cathie, 1995)

I also gleaned useful information from chocolatenecessities.com, cloudappreciationsociety.org, ecology.com, french.about.com and lightningsafety.noaa.gov.

# Index

# INDEX